FREE STUFF FOR KIDS

Our Pledge

We have collected and examined the best free and up-to-a-dollar offers we could find. Each supplier in this book has promised to honor properly made requests for **single items** through **2000**. Though mistakes do happen, we are doing our best to make sure this book really works.

—*The Free Stuff Editors*

Meadowbrook Press

Distributed by Simon & Schuster
New York

The Free Stuff Editors

Director: Bruce Lansky
Editor: Heather Hooper
Copywriter: Heather Hooper
Copy Editor: Melanie Mallon
Production Manager: Joe Gagne
Desktop Publishing: Danielle White

ISBN: 0-88166-344-1
Simon & Schuster Ordering # 0-689-82681-8

ISSN: 1056-9693
23rd Edition

Published by Meadowbrook Press, 5451 Smetana Drive, Minnetonka, MN 55343

www.meadowbrookpress.com

BOOK TRADE DISTRIBUTION by Simon & Schuster, a division of Simon and Schuster, Inc., 1230 Avenue of the Americas, New York, NY 10020.

00 99   5 4 3 2 1

Printed in the United States of America

Contents

Thank You's. iv
Read This First I
About This Book 2
Free Stuff for Kids Checklist . . 8

SPORTS
Basketball 10
Baseball. 12
Football. 15
Hockey 16
Trading Cards. 17
Olympic Sports 18
Outdoor Sports 19
Amateur Sports 20
Classic Sports. 21
Sport Accessories 22

JEWELRY
Bracelets. 24
Necklaces 27
Jewelry 28
Rings 30
Stick-On Jewelry 31
Fun Stuff 32

STICKERS AND TATTOOS
Stickers 34
Animal Stickers. 35

Special Effects Stickers. . . . 37
Miscellaneous Stickers 38
Tattoos 39

SCHOOL SUPPLIES AND ACTIVITIES
Rubber Stamps. 44
Rulers 45
Fun Packs 46
Erasers 47
Letter Writing. 48
Pencils and Pens 50
Stencils 52
Cool Stuff 53
Games 56

READING
Bookmarks 60
Book Stuff. 63
Activity Magazines 64
Comic Books 65
Personal Reading 66
Magazines 67
Writing 68

ENVIRONMENT
Newsletters 70
Animal Reading. 71

Animal Toys. 73
Trees 75
Stickers 76
Awareness 77
Seeds. 78

AWARENESS AND SELF-ESTEEM
Posters 80
Safety. 81
Magnets. 84
Self-Esteem 85
Letters. 86
Cool Stuff 87
Friends 88

WORLD CULTURE
Stamps. 90
Foreign Money 91
Chinese Stuff 92
Write a Letter 93
See the World. 94
Our Earth 96

THE INTERNET 97

INDEX 103

Thank You's

To Pat Blakely, Barbara Haislet, and Judith Hentges for creating and publishing the original *Rainbow Book*, proving that kids, parents, and teachers would respond enthusiastically to a source of free things by mail. They taught us the importance of carefully checking the quality of each item and doing our best to make sure that each and every request is satisfied.

Our heartfelt appreciation goes to hundreds of organizations and individuals for making this book possible. The suppliers and editors of this book have a common goal: to make it possible for kids to reach out and discover the world by themselves.

MEADOWBROOK PRESS

2000 EDITION

U.S. MAIL

ReaD THiS FiRST

About This Book

Free Stuff for Kids lists hundreds of items you can send away for. The Free Stuff Editors have examined every item and think each is among the best offers available. There are no trick offers—only safe, fun, and informative things you'll like!

This book is designed for kids who can read and write. The directions on the following pages explain exactly how to request an item. Read the instructions carefully so you know how to send a request. Making sure you've filled out a request correctly is easy—just complete the **Free Stuff for Kids Checklist** on page 8. Half the fun is using the book on your own. The other half is getting a real reward for your efforts!

Each year the Free Stuff Editors create a new edition of this book, taking out old items, inserting new ones, and changing addresses and prices. It is important for you to use an updated edition because the suppliers only honor properly made requests for single items for the **current** edition. If you use this edition after **2000**, your request will not be honored.

Reading Carefully

Read the descriptions of the offers carefully to find out exactly what you're getting. Here are some guidelines to help you know what you're sending for:

• A pamphlet is usually one sheet of paper folded over and printed on both sides.

• A booklet is usually larger than a pamphlet and contains more pages, but it's smaller than a book.

Following Directions

It's important to follow each supplier's directions. On one offer, you might need to use a postcard. On another offer, you might be asked to include money or a long self-addressed stamped envelope. If you do not follow the directions **exactly**, you might not get your request. Unless the directions tell you differently, ask for only **one** of anything you send for. Family or classroom members using the same book must send **separate** requests.

Sending Postcards

A postcard is a small card you can write on and send through the mail without an envelope. Many suppliers offering free items require you to send requests on postcards. Please do this. It saves them the time it takes to open many envelopes.

The post office sells postcards with preprinted postage. You can also buy postcards at a drugstore and put special postcard stamps on them yourself. Your local post office can tell you how much a postcard stamp currently costs. (Postcards with a picture on them are usually more expensive.) You must use a postcard that is at least 3½-by-5½-inches.) Your postcards should be addressed like the one below:

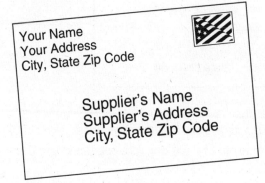

Your Name
Your Address
City, State Zip Code

Supplier's Name
Supplier's Address
City, State Zip Code

Dear Sir or Madam:

Please send me some super cool stuff. Thank you very much.

Sincerely,
Your Name
Your Address
City, State Zip Code

Front   Back

- **Neatly print** the supplier's address on the side of the postcard that has the postage. Put your return address in the upper left-hand corner of that side as well.
- **Neatly print** your request, your name, and your address on the blank side of the postcard.
- Do not abbreviate the name of your street or city.
- Use a ballpoint pen. Pencil can be difficult to read, and ink pens often smear.

Sending Letters

Your letters should look like the one below:

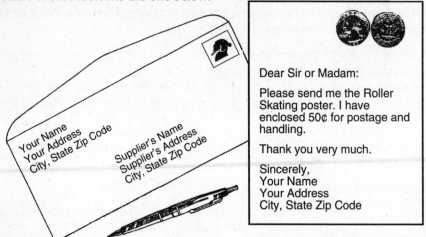

Dear Sir or Madam:

Please send me the Roller Skating poster. I have enclosed 50¢ for postage and handling.

Thank you very much.

Sincerely,
Your Name
Your Address
City, State Zip Code

- **Neatly print** the name of the item you want exactly as you see it in the directions.
- **Neatly print** your own name and address at the bottom of the letter. (Do not abbreviate the name of your street or city.)
- If you're including coins or a long self-addressed stamped envelope, say so in the letter. And be sure to enclose the coins and the envelope!
- Put a **first-class stamp** on any envelope you send. You can get stamps at the post office.
- **Neatly print** the supplier's address in the center of the envelope and your return address in the upper left-hand corner.
- If you're sending many letters at once, make sure you put the correct letter in the correct envelope.
- Use a ballpoint pen. Pencil can be difficult to read, and ink pens often smear.

Sending a Long Self-Addressed Stamped Envelope

If the directions say to enclose a long self-addressed stamped envelope, here's how to do it:

- **Neatly print** your name and address in the center of a **9½-inch-long envelope** as if you were mailing it to yourself. Print your return address in the upper left-hand corner of the envelope as well. Put a **first-class stamp** on it.

- **Fold up** (but don't seal!) the long self-addressed stamped envelope and put it inside another **9½-inch-long envelope** (along with your letter to the supplier). Put a **first-class stamp** on the second envelope, too.
- **Neatly print** the supplier's address in the center of the outside envelope and your return address in the upper left-hand corner.
- Use a ballpoint pen.

Sending Money

Many of the suppliers in this book are not charging you for their items. However, the cost of postage and handling is high today, and suppliers must charge you for this. If the directions say to enclose money, **you must do so.** Here are a few rules about sending money:

- Tape the coins to your letter or index card so they won't break out of the envelope.
- Don't stack your coins on top of each other in the envelope.
- Don't use pennies and avoid using nickels. These coins will add weight to your envelope, and you may need to use more than one stamp.
- If an item costs $1.00, send a one-dollar bill instead of coins. Don't tape dollar bills.
- Send only U.S. money.
- If a grown-up is helping you, he or she may write a check (unless the directions tell you not to send checks).
- Send all money directly to the suppliers—their addresses are listed with their offers.

Getting Your Stuff

Expect to wait **four to eight weeks** for your stuff to arrive. Sometimes you have to wait longer. Remember, suppliers get thousands of requests each year. Please be patient! If you wait a long time and your offer still doesn't come, you may be using the wrong edition. This is the **2000** edition—the offers in this book will only be good for 1999 and 2000!

Making Sure You Get Your Request

The Free Stuff Editors have tried to make the directions for using this book as clear as possible, to make sure you get what you send for. But you must follow **all** of the directions **exactly** as they're written, or the supplier **will not be able to answer your request**. If you're confused about the directions, ask a grown-up to help you.

Do's and Don'ts:

- **Do** use a ballpoint pen. Typing and using a computer are okay, too.
- **Do** print. Cursive can be difficult to read.
- **Do** print your name, address, and Zip code clearly and fully on the postcard or on the envelope **and** on the letter you send—sometimes envelopes and letters get separated after they reach the supplier.
- **Do** send the correct amount of U.S. money, but don't use pennies.
- **Do** tape the coins to the letter you send them with. If you don't tape them, the coins might rip the envelope and fall out.
- **Do** use a **9½-inch-long** self-addressed stamped envelope when the instructions ask for a "long" envelope.

INSTRUCTIONS

- **Do not** use this **2000** edition **after** 2000.
- **Do not** ask for more than **one** of an item, unless the directions say you can.
- **Do not** stack coins in the envelope.
- **Do not** seal your long self-addressed stamped envelope. The suppliers need to be able to put the item you ordered in the envelope you send.
- **Do not** ask Meadowbrook Press to send you any of the items listed in the book unless you are ordering the Meadowbrook offers from pages 61 and 63. The publishers of this book do not carry items belonging to other suppliers. They do not supply refunds, either.

Follow all the rules to avoid disappointment!

What to Do If You Aren't Satisfied:

If you have complaints about any offer, or if you don't receive the items you sent for within eight to ten weeks, contact the Free Stuff Editors. Before you complain, please reread the directions. Are you sure you followed them properly? Are you using this **2000** edition **after** 2000? (The offers in this book are only good for 1999 and 2000.) The Free Stuff Editors won't be able to send you the item, but they can make sure that any suppliers who don't fulfill requests are dropped from next year's *Free Stuff for Kids*. For **each** of your complaints you must tell us the name of the offer as it appears in the book, the page number of the offer, and the date you sent your request. Without this information, we may not be able to help you. We'd like to know which offers you like and what kind of new offers you'd like us to add to next year's edition. So don't be bashful—write us a letter. Send your complaints or suggestions to:

The Free Stuff Editors
Meadowbrook Press
5451 Smetana Drive
Minnetonka, MN 55343

Free Stuff for Kids Checklist

Use this checklist each time you send out a request. It will help you follow directions **exactly** and prevent mistakes. Put a check mark in the box each time you complete a task—you can photocopy this page and use it again and again.

For all requests:

❏ I sent my request during either **1999** or **2000**.

When sending postcards and letters:

❏ I used a ballpoint pen.

❏ I printed neatly and carefully.

❏ I asked for the correct item (only one).

❏ I wrote to the correct supplier.

❏ I double-checked the supplier's address.

When sending postcards only:

❏ I put my return address on the postcard.

❏ I applied a postcard stamp (if the postage wasn't preprnted).

When sending letters only:

❏ I put my return address on the letter.

❏ I included a **9½-inch-long** self-addressed stamped envelope (if the directions asked for one).

❏ I included the correct amount of money (if the directions asked for money).

❏ I put my return address on the envelope.

❏ I applied a **first-class stamp.**

When sending a long self-addressed stamped envelope:

❏ I used a **9½-inch-long** envelope.

❏ I put my address on the front of the envelope.

❏ I put my return address in the upper left-hand corner of the envelope.

❏ I left the envelope unsealed.

❏ I applied a **first-class stamp**.

When responding to one-dollar offers:

❏ I sent U.S. money.

❏ I enclosed a one-dollar bill with my letter instead of coins.

When sending coins:

❏ I sent U.S. money.

❏ I taped the coins to my letter or to an index card.

❏ I did not stack the coins on top of each other.

❏ I did not use pennies. (Extra coins make the envelope heavier and may require extra postage.)

MEADOWBROOK PRESS

2000
EDITION

U.S.
MAIL

SPORTS

BASKETBALL

Chicago Bulls

Charge! Get out of the bullpen for this amazing fan pack from the Chicago Bulls. You'll receive a fan letter, sticker, schedule, and fan club offer— no bull about it!

Directions:	Read and follow the instructions on pages 2-8. **Print** your request **neatly** on paper and put it in an envelope. You must enclose a **long self-addressed stamped envelope**.
Write to:	Chicago Bulls 1901 West Madison Chicago, IL 60612
Ask for:	Fan pack

Atlanta Hawks

Fly away with this exciting offer from the Atlanta Hawks. You'll receive a bumper sticker to put on your parents' car, your bike, or anywhere else you want to fly your pride!

Directions:	Read and follow the instructions on pages 2-8. **Print** your request **neatly** on paper and put it in an envelope. You must enclose a **long self-addressed stamped envelope**.
Write to:	Atlanta Hawks Re: Free Stuff for Kids One CNN Center, Ste. 405 Atlanta, GA 30303
Ask for:	Atlanta Hawks team bumper sticker

Detroit Pistons

Get fired up with the Detroit Pistons and receive this cool sticker with the Pistons' logo on it. You'll explode with team spirit!

Directions:	Read and follow the instructions on pages 2-8. Print your request neatly on paper and put it in an envelope. You must enclose a long self-addressed stamped envelope.
Write to:	Detroit Pistons 2 Championship Drive Auburn Hills, MI 48326
Ask for:	Sticker with Detroit Pistons logo

Detroit Shock

You'll be shocked by this offer from the WNBA's Detroit Shock. You'll receive a round sticker with the team's logo on it. It's electrifying!

Directions:	Read and follow the instructions on pages 2-8. Print your request neatly on paper and put it in an envelope. You must enclose a long self-addressed stamped envelope.
Write to:	Detroit Shock 2 Championship Drive Auburn Hills, MI 48326
Ask for:	Round Sticker with Detroit Shock logo

BASEBALL

Chicago White Sox

This offer will have you jumping out of your socks with excitement! You'll receive a sticker with the White Sox logo that you can put anywhere to let everyone know how much you love your team.

Kansas City Royals

You'll feel like royalty with this crown-jewel of an offer! This fan pack features a decal, a baseball card, and a photocard of Slugerr,—the Kansas City Royals' mascot.

Directions:	Read and follow the instructions on pages 2-8. Print your request neatly on paper and put it in an envelope. You must enclose a long self-addressed stamped envelope.
Write to:	Chicago White Sox 333 W. 35th Street Chicago, IL 60616
Ask for:	Sticker

Directions:	Read and follow the instructions on pages 2-8. Print your request neatly on paper and put it in an envelope. You must enclose a long self-addressed stamped envelope.
Write to:	Kansas City Royals P.O. Box 419969 Kansas City, MO 64141
Ask for:	Kansas City Royals fan pack

BASEBALL

Detroit Tigers

What a grrrrr-eat offer! This up-to-date Tigers fan pack will have you growling with team spirit. During the off season you will receive four players' photos. Clap your paws for the Tigers!

Directions:	Read and follow the instructions on pages 2-8. Print your request neatly on paper and put it in an envelope. You must enclose a long self-addressed stamped envelope.
Write to:	Detroit Tigers 2121 Trumbull Avenue Detroit, MI 48216
Ask for:	Fan Pack

Phillies

Pheel the Phillies' pride. You'll receive two player/coach photocards, a schedule, and a team picture. Philadelphia will welcome ya!

Directions:	Read and follow the instructions on pages 2-8. Print your request neatly on paper and put it in an envelope. You must enclose a long self-addressed stamped envelope.
Write to:	Phillies P.O. Box 7575 Philadelphia, PA 19101
Ask for:	Fan pack

Prince William Cannons

You'll be booming with excitement for this offer! The Cannons are a minor league team with major talent. So fire up the cannons with this awesome sticker.

WINCRAFT PBGOMLB 1996

Directions:	**Read and follow the instructions on pages 2-8. Print** your request **neatly** on paper and put it in an envelope. You must enclose a **long self-addressed stamped envelope.**
Write to:	Prince William Cannons P.O. Box 2148 Woodbride, VA 22193
Ask for:	Sticker

Durham Bulls

Get charged up with a Durham Bulls fan pack. You'll receive a pocket schedule, a Wool E. Bull mascot card, a souvenir store catalog, and a player card.

Directions:	**Read and follow the instructions on pages 2-8. Print** your request **neatly** on paper and put it in an envelope. You must enclose a **long self-addressed stamped envelope.**
Write to:	Durham Bulls Baseball Club 409 Blackwell Street Durham, NC 27701
Ask for:	Fan Pack

Buffalo Bills

Rope yourself a little of the Wild West with the Buffalo Bills. You'll receive a current team photo and a helmet logo sticker. Join the stampede!

Directions:	Read and follow the instructions on pages 2-8. **Print** your request **neatly** on paper and put it in an envelope. You must enclose a **long self-addressed stamped envelope.**
Write to:	Buffalo Bills One Bills Drive Orchard Park, NY 14217
Ask for:	Fan pack

Football Cards

Kick a field goal with an unopened pack of football cards from 1993 or earlier. This is a great way to get any football cards you may have missed, or to start a new collection!

Directions:	Read and follow the instructions on pages 2-8. **Print** your request **neatly** on paper and put it in an envelope. You must enclose a **long self-addressed stamped envelope** and **75¢.**
Write to:	Sayre's Route 2, Box 46B1 Letart, WV 25253
Ask for:	Football cards

Chicago Blackhawks

Soar with the hawks! If you love hawk-ey, you'll love this fan pack, which includes a schedule, a decal, and three player cards. Fly with a great team.

Directions:	Read and follow the instructions on pages 2-8. Print your request neatly on paper and put it in an envelope. You must enclose a long self-addressed stamped envelope.
Write to:	Chicago Blackhawks Hockey Team 1901 W. Madison Street Chicago, IL 60612
Ask for:	Fan pack

Buffalo Sabres

Check it out! You can be a member of Sabre Kids, the Buffalo Sabres Kids' Club when you send for the information and application to join.

Directions:	Read and follow the instructions on pages 2-8. Print your request neatly on paper and put it in an envelope.
Write to:	Buffalo Sabres One Seymour H. Knox III Plaza Buffalo, NY 14203
Ask for:	Membership in Sabre Kids

Trading Cards

If you can't decide whether football, basketball, baseball, or hockey is your favorite sport, this offer is perfect for you. The sports nut in you will love it.

Comical Cards

You'll be Looney with these cards! Each card features one of your favorite Looney Tunes characters and a well-known athlete along with fun trivia questions on the back. Daffy and the gang love sports as much as you!

Directions:	Read and follow the instructions on pages 2-8. **Print** your request **neatly** on paper and put it in an envelope. You must enclose a **long self-addressed stamped envelope.**
Write to:	Quad Star Sports 2 Bradbury Circle P.O. Box 7561 Lawton, OK 73506
Ask for:	Four free sports trading cards

Directions:	Read and follow the instructions on pages 2-8. **Print** your request **neatly** on paper and put it in an envelope. You must enclose a **long self-addressed stamped envelope** and **75¢.**
Write to:	Sayre's Route 2, Box 46B1 Letart, WV 25253
Ask for:	Pack of comic ball cards

USA Gymnastics

You and your friends will flip out when you receive this *Guide to Gymnastics* booklet. You'll be beaming—guaranteed!

Directions:	Read and follow the instructions on pages 2-8. Print your request neatly on paper and put it in an envelope.
Write to:	USA Gymnastics 201 S. Capitol Avenue Suite 300 Indianapolis, IN 46225
Ask for:	Guide to Gymnastics booklet

USA Swimming

This official USA Swimming decal is sure to make a splash among your swimming buddies. Don't wade, send for it now!

Directions:	Read and follow the instructions on pages 2-8. Print your request neatly on paper and put it in an envelope. You must enclose a **long self-addressed stamped envelope**.
Write to:	USA Swimming One Olympic Plaza Colorado Springs, CO 80909
Ask for:	USA Swimming decal

Canoe and Kayak

Don't throw in the paddle—learn how to be safe in a canoe or kayak. This safety education pamphlet will tell you how to have fun in the water and be safe, too! If you don't want to be swimming with questions, send for this pamphlet.

Directions:	Read and follow the instructions on pages **2-8**. **Print** your request **neatly** on paper and put it in an envelope. You must enclose a **long self-addressed stamped envelope.**
Write to:	United States Canoe Association, Inc. P.O. Box 5743 Lafayette, IN 47903
Ask for:	Canoeing and kayaking safety education pamphlet

Horseback Riding

If you love horses, you'll love this horse activity book, poster, and bumper sticker. So saddle up, partner, and get ready to ride!

Directions:	Read and follow the instructions on pages **2-8**. **Print** your request **neatly** on paper and put it in an envelope.
Write to:	American Quarter Horse Association P.O. Box 200 Amarillo, TX 79168
Ask for:	Horse activity book, poster, and bumper sticker

19

Amateur Athletics

Do you love sports but aren't quite ready for the pros? Then send for this information from the Amateur Athletic Union and find out about the different kinds of sports you can play.

Directions:	Read and follow the instructions on pages 2-8. Print your request neatly on paper and put it in an envelope. You must enclose a long self-addressed stamped envelope.
Write to:	Amateur Athletic Union ATTN: Sports Program Department c/o Walt Disney World Resort P.O. Box 10,000 Lake Buena Vista, FL 32830-1000
Ask for:	*AAU Sports Program* brochure

Roller Skating

Rock 'n' roll with a kids' skating kit from the Roller Skating Association International. You'll receive a poster, a trading card, an inline skating tip booklet, and a letter from Roller Roo himself.

Directions:	Read and follow the instructions on pages 2-8. Print your request neatly on paper and put it in an envelope. You must enclose $1.00.
Write to:	Roller Skating Association International 6905 Corporate Drive Indianapolis, IN 46278
Ask for:	Kids' skating kit

Fencing

Learn about the ancient sport of fencing. You'll receive a welcome packet and a USFA sticker. So don't straddle the fence—send for this offer today.

Directions:	Read and follow the instructions on pages 2-8. Print your request neatly on paper and put it in an envelope. You must enclose a **long self-addressed stamped envelope** and **50¢.**
Write to:	United States Fencing Association One Olympic Plaza Colorado Springs, CO 80909
Ask for:	Welcome packet and USFA sticker

USA Badminton

These birdies don't sing, but they sure do fly! Badminton is actually the world's fastest racquet sport. Send for this magnet and learn more about the exciting sport of badminton.

Directions:	Read and follow the instructions on pages 2-8. Print your request neatly on paper and put it in an envelope.
Write to:	USA Badminton Olympic Training Center One Olympic Plaza Colorado Springs, CO 80909
Ask for:	USA Badminton magnet

Soccer Stuff

Score a goal with this soccer magnet and ID tag. Put a picture of your favorite soccer star in the frame and let everyone know you are a fan of the most popular sport in the world!

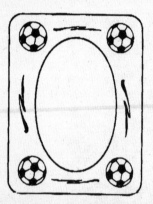

Sports Ball Erasers

Show your love of sports in the classroom with these sports ball erasers. You'll receive a soccer ball, football, basketball, and baseball. While they're too little to actually play with, these balls are still loads of fun!

Directions:	Read and follow the instructions on pages 2-8. Print your request neatly on paper and put it in an envelope. You must enclose a long self-addressed stamped envelope and $1.00.
Write to:	S & D Dept. M P.O. Box 114 Casey, IL 62420
Ask for:	Soccer magnet and frame

Directions:	Read and follow the instructions on pages 2-8. Print your request neatly on paper and put it in an envelope. You must enclose a long self-addressed stamped envelope and 35¢.
Write to:	Daisy Enterprises Dept. SBE P.O. Box 1426 Rutherfordton, NC 28139
Ask for:	Four sports ball erasers

MEADOWBROOK PRESS **2000 EDITION**

U.S. MAIL

JEWELRY

Springy Neon Bracelet

This bracelet is springy, sprongy, and comes in a bright neon color you can see across a room! How can you not be glamorous with this on your wrist? Plus, it's fun to play with!

Directions:	Read and follow the instructions on pages 2-8. **Print** your request **neatly** on paper and put it in an envelope. You must enclose a **long self-addressed stamped envelope** and **50¢**.
Write to:	Daisy Enterprises Dept. SPBT P.O. Box 1426 Rutherfordton, NC 28139
Ask for:	Springy neon bracelet

Glitter Bracelet

You'll look absolutely fabulous as you sparkle like the stars! The glitter in this bracelet can light up a room better than a disco ball! You'll receive one clear bracelet with moving glitter inside of it.

Directions:	Read and follow the instructions on pages 2-8. **Print** your request **neatly** on paper and put it in an envelope. You must enclose a **long self-addressed stamped envelope** and **$1.00**.
Write to:	Daisy Enterprises Dept. GBT P.O. Box 1426 Rutherfordton, NC 28139
Ask for:	Glitter bracelet

Glass Bead Bracelet

You'll bead the only kid on your block to have a bracelet like this. Each bracelet is made out of beautiful glass-like beads. Positively stunning!

Directions:	Read and follow the instructions on pages 2-8. Print your request neatly on paper and put it in an envelope. You must enclose a long self-addressed stamped envelope and 75¢.
Write to:	Daisy Enterprises Dept. GBB P.O. Box 1426 Rutherfordton, NC 28139
Ask for:	Glass bead bracelet

Foam Smiley Face

Share a smile with everyone around you! This bright yellow happy face bracelet will spread more sunshine than the sun. Don't worry, be happy!

Directions:	Read and follow the instructions on pages 2-8. Print your request neatly on paper and put it in an envelope. You must enclose a long self-addressed stamped envelope and 75¢.
Write to:	Daisy Enterprises Dept. FSB P.O. Box 1426 Rutherfordton, NC 28139
Ask for:	Foam smiley face bracelet

Macramé Bracelet

Make your own macramé bracelet. This kit contains materials and instructions needed to make one beaded macramé bracelet. It's easy and looks awesome!

Directions:	Read and follow the instructions on pages **2-8**. **Print** your request **neatly** on paper and put it in an envelope. You must enclose a **long self-addressed stamped envelope** and **$1.00**.
Write to:	Grin 'N Barrett 1227 S. Muirfield Road—M Los Angeles, CA 90019-3040
Ask for:	Beaded macramé bracelet

Friendship Bracelet

Wear and share this friendship bracelet. You will receive two bracelets—one for you and one for your friend—to show that you'll be friends forever. Each bracelet is made of colorful yarn and looks great!

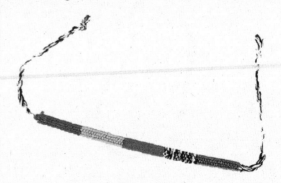

Directions:	Read and follow the instructions on pages **2-8**. **Print** your request **neatly** on paper and put it in an envelope. You must enclose a **long self-addressed stamped envelope** and **$1.00**.
Write to:	Phil Labush 9360 Northwest 39th Street Sunrise, FL 33351
Ask for:	Friendship bracelet

Troll Necklace

These wild and crazy trolls just love to hang around people—around their necks, that is. These troll necklaces have wild and crazy hair, and if you're a wild and crazy kid, you might just make a new friend!

Directions:	Read and follow the instructions on pages 2-8. Print your request neatly on paper and put it in an envelope. You must enclose a long self-addressed stamped envelope and $1.00.
Write to:	Surprise Gift of the Month Club P.O. Box 1 Stony Point, NY 10980
Ask for:	Norfin troll necklace

Best Buds

Your best bud will love a part of this frog necklace. You'll receive one necklace split in two so that you can give one half to your best friend and wear the other half yourself. When you put the necklaces together, they match perfectly—just like you and your friend!

Directions:	Read and follow the instructions on pages 2-8. Print your request neatly on paper and put it in an envelope. You must enclose a long self-addressed stamped envelope and $1.00.
Write to:	Phil Labush 9360 Northwest 39th Street Sunrise, FL 33351
Ask for:	Frog necklace

Alien Necklace

Visitors from another planet will notice your new alien necklace. This offer is larger than the galaxy, brighter than the sun, and cooler than the surface of the moon.

Directions:	Read and follow the instructions on pages 2-8. **Print** your request **neatly** on paper and put it in an envelope. You must enclose a **long self-addressed stamped envelope** and **$1.00.**
Write to:	Daisy Enterprises Dept. AN P.O. Box 1426 Rutherfordton, NC 28139
Ask for:	Alien necklace

Alien Ring

Get an alien ring to match your alien necklace and be truly far out! You'll receive one ring with an alien head on it.

Directions:	Read and follow the instructions on pages 2-8. **Print** your request **neatly** on paper and put it in an envelope. You must enclose a **long self-addressed stamped envelope** and **50¢.**
Write to:	Phil Labush 9360 Northwest 39th Street Sunrise, FL 33351
Ask for:	Alien ring

Ring and Earring Set

Be a movie star for a day with these stick-on earrings and silver glitter flower ring. They match perfectly!

Crystal Kit

Design your own jewelry! Each kit contains the materials and instructions necessary to make an original and gorgeous piece of jewelry. You can choose from necklaces, barrettes, or rings. They're easy to make and a lot of fun.

Directions:	Read and follow the instructions on pages 2-8. Print your request neatly on paper and put it in an envelope. You must enclose a long self-addressed stamped envelope and $1.00.
Write to:	Daisy Enterprises Dept. RES P.O. Box 1426 Rutherfordton, NC 28139
Ask for:	Ring and earring set

Directions:	Read and follow the instructions on pages 2-8. Print your request neatly on paper and put it in an envelope. You must enclose a long self-addressed stamped envelope with two stamps and $1.00.
Write to:	Grin 'N Barrett, Code C 1227 Muirfield Road Los Angeles, CA 90019-3040
Ask for:	Baked crystal kit (specify necklace, barrettes, or rings)

Awesome Offer

Gold Rings

These rings are spectacular! You'll get three gold-plated rings. Of course they aren't real gold, but they shine like they are! Your fingers will be gorgeous.

Directions:	**Read and follow the instructions on pages 2-8. Print** your request **neatly** on paper and put it in an envelope. You must enclose a **long self-addressed stamped envelope** and **50¢.**
Write to:	Phil Labush 9360 Northwest 39th Street Sunrise, FL 33351
Ask for:	Gold-plated laser-cut rings

Virtual Pet Ring

Who says you can't bring your pet with you to school? This virtual ring can travel with you anywhere. It changes images every time you move your finger so it looks like your dog is really wagging its tail at you! There are assorted pets and designs.

Directions:	**Read and follow the instructions on pages 2-8. Print** your request **neatly** on paper and put it in an envelope. You must enclose a **long self-addressed stamped envelope** and **75¢.**
Write to:	Daisy Enterprises Dept. FKRN P.O. Box 1426 Rutherfordton, NC 28139
Ask for:	Virtual pet ring

Stick-On Earrings

Change your earrings every day of the month, even if your ears aren't pierced! You'll get a calendar with a different pair of stick-on earrings for each day!

Stick-On Stones

You'll sparkle and shine with these stick-on stones. You can stick them on your face, your ears, your fingernails, or anywhere you want! You'll be smashing!

Directions:	Read and follow the instructions on pages 2-8. Print your request neatly on paper and put it in an envelope. You must enclose a long self-addressed stamped envelope and $1.00.
Write to:	Alvin Peters Company Dept. GJ P.O. Box 2050 Albany, NY 12220-0050
Ask for:	Thirty pairs of stick-on earrings

Directions:	Read and follow the instructions on pages 2-8. Print your request neatly on paper and put it in an envelope. You must enclose a long self-addressed stamped envelope and $1.00.
Write to:	Winslow Publishing P.O. Box 38012 Toronto, ON M5N 3A8 Canada
Ask for:	Stick-on stones

Twisted Shoelaces

Do the twist! These shoelaces are a twisted and fun way to make your shoes look great. You'll receive two shoelaces in bright neon colors. They're so twisted you don't even need to tie them! Specify green, pink, yellow, or orange.

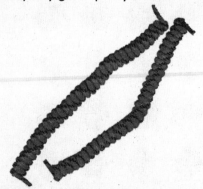

Directions:	Read and follow the instructions on pages 2-8. Print your request neatly on paper and put it in an envelope. You must enclose a long self-addressed stamped envelope and $1.00. *No checks please.*
Write to:	KittyCo Dept. 201 P.O. Box 400 Scurry, TX 75158
Ask for:	Nylon neon twist shoelaces

Flower Pearl Earrings

These flower pearl earrings are fun to make and look really good! What more could you ask for in a pair of earrings? This kit contains all the materials and instructions necessary to make two pairs of ravishing earrings!

Directions:	Read and follow the instructions on pages 2-8. Print your request neatly on paper and put it in an envelope. You must enclose a long self-addressed stamped envelope and $1.00.
Write to:	Grin 'N Barrett, Code P 1227 S. Muirfield Road Los Angeles, CA 90019-3040
Ask for:	Flower pearl earring set

MEADOWBROOK PRESS
2000 EDITION

U.S. MAIL

STICKERS AND TATTOOS

Glow-in-the-Dark

When you turn the lights off you'll be seeing elephants. That's right! These stickers glow in the dark. You will also receive stickers with kittens, fish, and an octopus. Lights out!

Directions:	Read and follow the instructions on pages 2-8. Print your request neatly on paper and put it in an envelope. You must enclose **$1.00.**
Write to:	Stickers 'N Stuff P.O. Box 43, Dept. 2-GLO Louisville, CO 80027
Ask for:	Two sheets of glow-in-the-dark stickers

Who Rules?

Girls rule! Boys rule! Who rules? Everybody rules! With this offer you'll receive three stickers to put on your notebook or locker. Be sure to tell them whether you want boys or girls stickers.

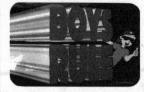

Directions:	Read and follow the instructions on pages 2-8. Print your request neatly on paper and put it in an envelope. You must enclose a **long self-addressed stamped envelope** and **50¢.**
Write to:	Daisy Enterprises Dept. Boy or Girl P.O. Box 1426 Rutherfordton, NC 28139
Ask for:	Boys or Girls Rule stickers

Barnyard Animals

These animals look so real you could create your own barnyard with them! You'll receive a sheet of stickers including twelve farm animals. They're practically mooing, baaing, gobbling, and barking off the paper!

Wild Cats

These prismatic stickers look wild and ferocious. You'll receive a sheet of stickers with different wildcats on it. You'll be the king or queen of the jungle with these stickers on your stuff.

Directions:	Read and follow the instructions on pages 2-8. **Print** your request **neatly** on paper and put it in an envelope. You must enclose a **long self-addressed stamped envelope** and **50¢**.
Write to:	Daisy Enterprises Dept. FS P.O. Box 1426 Rutherfordton, NC 28139
Ask for:	Farm animal stickers

Directions:	Read and follow the instructions on pages 2-8. **Print** your request **neatly** on paper and put it in an envelope. You must enclose a **long self-addressed stamped envelope** and **$1.00**.
Write to:	Winslow Publishing P.O. Box 38012 550 Eglinton Avenue West Toronto, ON M5N 3A8 Canada
Ask for:	Prismatic big cats stickers

No Fur!

Liberate a lobster, cut out dissection, and let everyone know how you feel about fur. You'll be a friend to animals and standing up for your beliefs. That's pretty cool for a sticker!

Directions:	Read and follow the instructions on pages 2-8. **Print** your request **neatly** on paper and put it in an envelope.
Write to:	PETA Education Department 501 Front Street Norfolk, VA 23510
Ask for:	Sheet of "No Fur" stickers, "Cut Out Dissection" sticker, and a lobster liberation sticker

Under the Sea

Now you can have an aquarium on the front of your notebook. You'll receive a sheet of beautiful sea life stickers complete with unusual animals from the bottom of the ocean. Brave the waves!

Directions:	Read and follow the instructions on pages 2-8. **Print** your request **neatly** on paper and put it in an envelope. You must enclose a **long self-addressed stamped envelope** and **75¢.**
Write to:	Alvin Peters Company Dept. 99SLPS P.O. Box 2050 Albany, NY 12220-0050
Ask for:	Sea life prism stickers

Oilies

These stickers change colors before your very eyes. Just touch the stickers and watch them become a rainbow of color! Great for decorating your stuff!

Directions:	Read and follow the instructions on pages 2-8. **Print** your request **neatly** on paper and put it in an envelope. You must enclose a **long self-addressed stamped envelope** and **$1.00**.
Write to:	Edinboro Creations, Dept. OLE 1210 Brierly Lane Munhall, PA 15120
Ask for:	Touch Me! Oilies stickers

Looney Tunes

Go looney tooney with all your favorite pals. You'll receive a sheet of Looney Tunes stickers to share with your friends or to keep for yourself. They're so tiny and toony, you can't help but love them!

TM & © 1994 WARNER BROS.

Directions:	Read and follow the instructions on pages 2-8. **Print** your request **neatly** on paper and put it in an envelope. You must enclose a **long self-addressed stamped envelope** and **75¢**.
Write to:	Alvin Peters Company Dept. 99LTPS P.O. Box 2050 Albany, NY 12220-0050
Ask for:	Looney Tunes stickers

Valu-Pack Stickers

If you can't decide what type of stickers you like best, this value pack will let you sample them all! You'll receive scratch-and-sniff stickers, fuzzy stickers, and shiny stickers, just to name a few!

Directions:	Read and follow the instructions on pages 2-8. Print your request neatly on paper and put it in an envelope. You must enclose 75¢.
Write to:	Mr. Rainbows P.O. Box 908 Dept. FS-66 Rio Grande, NJ 08242
Ask for:	Valu-pack stickers

Sports Ball Stickers

Fan is short for fanatic, and if you're a true sports fanatic, you'll want these sports ball stickers. You'll receive a sheet of three sets of four different stickers.

Directions:	Read and follow the instructions on pages 2-8. Print your request neatly on paper and put it in an envelope. You must enclose a long self-addressed stamped envelope and 75¢.
Write to:	Alvin Peters Company Dept. 99SBPS P.O. Box 2050 Albany, NY 12220-0050
Ask for:	Sports ball stickers

Treasure Trolls

These trolls aren't the scary trolls that live under bridges waiting to scare you—they're actually cute tattoos! They're guaranteed to be friendly with their awesome hair!

Directions:	Read and follow the instructions on pages 2-8. Print your request neatly on paper and put it in an envelope. You must enclose a long self-addressed stamped envelope and 75¢.
Write to:	Alvin Peters Company Dept. TTRT P.O. Box 2050 Albany, NY 12220-0050
Ask for:	Treasure troll tattoos

Alien Tattoos

This offer is out of this world! You'll receive two different tattoos. Wear these tattoos and let everyone know—especially visitors from another planet—that you come in peace.

Directions:	Read and follow the instructions on pages 2-8. Print your request neatly on paper and put it in an envelope. You must enclose a long self-addressed stamped envelope and 50¢.
Write to:	Alvin Peters Company Dept. 99AT P.O. Box 2050 Albany, NY 12220-0050
Ask for:	Alien tattoos

Groovy Tattoos

Peace, man. Find your center, spread love and happiness, and wear these tattoos. Your parents will love you for it! These tattoos are far out!

Glow-in-the-Dark

You'll be glowing when you wear these tattoos! You will receive a variety of tattoos, all glowingly great!

Directions:	Read and follow the instructions on pages 2-8. Print your request neatly on paper and put it in an envelope. You must enclose a long self-addressed stamped envelope and 50¢.
Write to:	Alvin Peters Company Dept. 9845-FK P.O. Box 2050 Albany, NY 12220-0050
Ask for:	'60s tattoos

Directions:	Read and follow the instructions on pages 2-8. Print your request neatly on paper and put it in an envelope. You must enclose a 6x9 self-addressed stamped envelope and $1.00.
Write to:	Alvin Peters Company Dept. 99 Glow-in-the-Dark Tattoos P.O. Box 2050 Albany, NY 12220-0050
Ask for:	Glow-in-the-dark tattoos

Hockey Tattoos

Score a goal! You'll receive two hockey tattoos to wear to all your hockey games! This offer is n-ice!

Directions:	Read and follow the instructions on pages 2-8. Print your request neatly on paper and put it in an envelope. You must enclose a long self-addressed stamped envelope and 50¢.
Write to:	Alvin Peters Company Dept. 99HT P.O. Box 2050 Albany, NY 12220-0050
Ask for:	Hockey tattoos

Cute Tattoos

These tattoos are positively adorable. Kittens, clowns, and teddy bears are just some of the tattoos you will receive. They're too cute!

Directions:	Read and follow the instructions on pages 2-8. Print your request neatly on paper and put it in an envelope. You must enclose a long self-addressed stamped envelope and $1.00.
Write to:	Winslow Publishing P.O. Box 38012 550 Eglinton Avenue West Toronto, ON M5N 3A8 Canada
Ask for:	Animal tattoos

Animaniacs

Be a maniac with the Animaniacs. You'll receive two Animaniac tattoos that are as funny and cute as the characters on the TV show. Be a part of the Animania mania!

Directions:	Read and follow the instructions on pages 2-8. **Print** your request **neatly** on paper and put it in an envelope. You must enclose a **long self-addressed stamped envelope** and **50¢.**
Write to:	Alvin Peters Company Dept. 99AT P.O. Box 2050 Albany, NY 12220-0050
Ask for:	Animaniac tattoos

Nail Decos

These nail decos are a great alternative to nail polish. You'll receive seven days worth of fun nail tattoos featuring flowers, frogs, and fruit. What a great way to spice up a week!

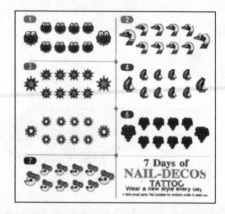

7 Days of
NAIL-DECOS
TATTOO
Wear a new style every day

Directions:	Read and follow the instructions on pages 2-8. **Print** your request **neatly** on paper and put it in an envelope. You must enclose a **long self-addressed stamped envelope** and **$1.00.**
Write to:	Phil Labush 9360 Northwest 39th Street Sunrise, FL 33351
Ask for:	7-day nail deco tattoos

MEADOWBROOK PRESS
2000 EDITION

U.S. MAIL

SCHOOL SUPPLIES AND ACTIVITIES

Cute Stamps

Stomp with excitement with these ink stamps. They're perfect for decorating your letters, notebooks, and tests—well, maybe not your tests. These cute animal stamps will make all of your stuff look adorable.

Directions:	**Read and follow the instructions on pages 2-8. Print** your request **neatly** on paper and put it in an envelope. You must enclose **$1.00.**
Write to:	Ramastamps 7924 Soper Hill Road Everett, WA 98205-1250
Ask for:	Two surprise stamps

Dinosaur Stamp

Who says dinosaurs are extinct? Now you can bring them back to life and into your school by using this dinosaur stamp. Plus, it's a self-inking stamp—the stamp and the ink come together in the same container. If you like dinosaurs, you'll love this.

Directions:	**Read and follow the instructions on pages 2-8. Print** your request **neatly** on paper and put it in an envelope. You must enclose a **6x9 self-addressed stamped envelope** and **75¢.**
Write to:	Alvin Peters Company Dept. 99DRS P.O. Box 2050 Albany, NY 12220-0050
Ask for:	Dino rubber stamper

Awesome Offer

Flicker Ruler

This groovy ruler changes images with a flick of the wrist. First you'll see the dinosaurs eating, then standing, then fighting. You won't believe your eyes! It's way cool!

Directions:	Read and follow the instructions on pages 2-8. **Print** your request **neatly** on paper and put it in an envelope. You must enclose a **long self-addressed stamped envelope** and 85¢.
Write to:	S.A.F.E. P.O. Box 40 1594 Brooklyn, NY 11240-1594
Ask for:	Dinosaur flicker ruler

Animal Ruler

There's a monkey climbing your ruler! No wait, it's just a monkey on your ruler. This ruler also has a built in magnifying glass. You can choose from a monkey, panda, lion, or alligator design. Go bananas!

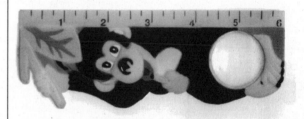

Directions:	Read and follow the instructions on pages 2-8. **Print** your request **neatly** on paper and put it in an envelope. You must enclose a **long self-addressed stamped envelope** and 75¢. *No checks please.*
Write to:	Michele Williams The Goody Box P.O. Box 400 Scurry, TX 75158
Ask for:	Animal magnifier rulers

Tropical Pack

Now you can have a little bit of the tropics in your backpack on cold, wintry days. You'll receive a cool notebook, three tattoos, three stickers, and two colorful fish erasers. So get ready to go swimming in this ocean of an offer!

Dalmatians

You'll be seeing spots when you open this pack of 101 Dalmatians. There aren't actually 101, but there's plenty to keep you barking for more! You'll receive two adorable erasers, three stickers, and three tattoos.

Directions:	Read and follow the instructions on pages 2-8. Print your request neatly on paper and put it in an envelope. You must enclose a long self-addressed stamped envelope and $1.00.
Write to:	Daisy Enterprises Dept. TP P.O. Box 1426 Rutherfordton, NC 28139
Ask for:	Tropical pack

Directions:	Read and follow the instructions on pages 2-8. Print your request neatly on paper and put it in an envelope. You must enclose a long self-addressed stamped envelope and $1.00.
Write to:	Daisy Enterprises Dept. DP2 P.O. Box 1426 Rutherfordton, NC 28139
Ask for:	Dalmatian pack

Crazy Daisies

These erasers are flowing with flower power. You'll spread peace, love, and happiness to all when you use these adorable smiley face daisies to erase any negative vibes (like a bad grade).

Directions:	**Read and follow the instructions on pages 2-8. Print** your request **neatly** on paper and put it in an envelope. You must enclose a **long self-addressed stamped envelope** and **35¢**.
Write to:	Daisy Enterprises Dept. SDE P.O. Box 1426 Rutherfordton, NC 28139
Ask for:	Smiley face daisy erasers

Stacking People

This offer is a pyramid of perfect fun! You'll receive six smiley face people erasers that really stack into a pyramid. Plus, they come in a whole rainbow of colors!

Directions:	**Read and follow the instructions on pages 2-8. Print** your request **neatly** on paper and put it in an envelope. You must enclose a **long self-addressed stamped envelope** and **50¢**.
Write to:	Daisy Enterprises Dept. SSPE P.O. Box 1426 Rutherfordton, NC 28139
Ask for:	Stacking smiley face people erasers

Wildlife Envelopes

Put the call of the wild into your letter-writing routine. These ferociously cool envelopes have pictures of different animals and exotic places, so the outside of your mail will be as interesting as the inside. Each envelope is die cut from a nature magazine, so you're also recycling!

Directions:	Read and follow the instructions on pages 2-8. **Print** your request **neatly** on paper and put it in an envelope. You must enclose **$1.00.**
Write to:	Alaska Craft Box 11-1102 Anchorage, AK 99511-1102
Ask for:	Wildlife envelopes

Fun Paper

Bug your friends and teacher with this cool paper. You'll receive five assorted sheets with bug designs, or five assorted sheets with animal skin designs, like a leopard, zebra, or snake.

Directions:	Read and follow the instructions on pages 2-8. **Print** your request **neatly** on paper and put it in an envelope. You must enclose **$1.00.**
Write to:	Winslow Publishing P.O. Box 38012 550 Eglinton Avenue West Toronto, ON M5N 3A8 Canada
Ask for:	Specify bug paper **or** animal skins paper

Stationery

Write to your pen pals on this pretty stationery. You'll get decorated paper and envelopes. All you need now are some stamps! Even writing to your great aunts will be fun with this beautiful stationery.

Directions:	Read and follow the instructions on pages 2-8. **Print** your request **neatly** on paper and put it in an envelope. You must enclose a **long self-addressed stamped envelope** and **$1.00**
Write to:	The Surprise Gift of the Month Club P.O. Box 1 Stony Point, NY 10980
Ask for:	Stationery

Animal Notepads

Whether you are a cat, dog, or horse lover, this notepad is a sure hit! Be sure you specify which one you want. Perfect to draw on when it's raining cats and dogs.

Directions:	Read and follow the instructions on pages 2-8. **Print** your request **neatly** on paper and put it in an envelope. You must enclose a **long self-addressed stamped envelope** and **$1.00**.
Write to:	Winslow Publishing P.O. Box 38012 550 Eglinton Avenue West Toronto, ON M5N 3A8 Canada
Ask for:	Animal notepads (specify kittens, puppies, or horses)

Scented Pencils

What's that smell? Chocolate, in a classroom? Fruit, during a test? It can't be possible. Well, it isn't real chocolate or fruit but these scented pencils smell so real they may be able to tide you over until lunch!

Directions:	Read and follow the instructions on pages 2-8. Print your request neatly on paper and put it in an envelope. You must enclose a long self-addressed stamped envelope and $1.00.
Write to:	Daisy Enterprises Dept. FSP (fruit) or CSP (chocolate) P.O. Box 1426 Rutherfordton, NC 28139
Ask for:	Fruit-scented pencil or chocolate-scented pencil

Space Pencil

Go for the stars with this spacey pencil. The planets, spaceships, and galaxies on the pencil will transport you to a galaxy far, far away. May the force be with you!

Directions:	Read and follow the instructions on pages 2-8. Print your request neatly on paper and put it in an envelope. You must enclose a long self-addressed stamped envelope and 50¢.
Write to:	Daisy Enterprises Dept. SP2 P.O. Box 1426 Rutherfordton, NC 28139
Ask for:	Space pencil

Fimo Clay Pencil

You've seen necklaces made out of fimo beads, but have you ever seen a pencil? This pencil is a guaranteed original. You'll be the only one with a pencil exactly like this because each pencil has a variety of fimo clay prints, so it would be impossible for any two to be exactly alike.

Directions:	Read and follow the instructions on pages 2-8. **Print** your request **neatly** on paper and put it in an envelope. You must enclose a **long self-addressed stamped envelope** and **50¢**.
Write to:	Daisy Enterprises Dept. FCP P.O. Box 1426 Rutherfordton, NC 28139
Ask for:	Fimo clay design pencil

Glitter Pen

This pen gives the Star-Spangled Banner a whole new meaning—it's positively spangled with glitter! You may also receive other pen designs that are equally as sparkly. This offer is truly cooly!

Directions:	Read and follow the instructions on pages 2-8. **Print** your request **neatly** on paper and put it in an envelope. You must enclose a **long self-addressed stamped envelope** and **$1.00**.
Write to:	Phil Labush 9360 Northwest 39th Street Sunrise, FL 33351
Ask for:	Laser cut pen

Dinosaur Stencil

Help! The dinosaurs are back! The dinosaurs are back—to school, that is, when you stencil them all over your notebooks. Each stencil has five different dinosaurs to draw. Be careful, though, they may bite!

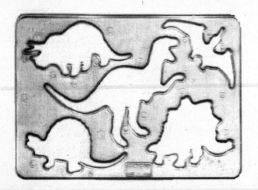

Directions:	Read and follow the instructions on pages 2-8. **Print** your request **neatly** on paper and put it in an envelope. You must enclose a **long self-addressed stamped envelope** and **75¢**.
Write to:	Alvin Peters Company Dept. 99DDS P.O. Box 2050 Albany, NY 12220-0050
Ask for:	Dinosaur stencil set

Animal Spiral Stencil

You'll be whirling and swirling with this animal stencil. They come in four assorted cute animal designs. You also get two spiral wheels that you can use to make lots of fun and exciting patterns.

Directions:	Read and follow the instructions on pages 2-8. **Print** your request **neatly** on paper and put it in an envelope. You must enclose a **long self-addressed stamped envelope** and **50¢**.
Write to:	Daisy Enterprises Dept. SA P.O. Box 1426 Rutherfordton, NC 28139
Ask for:	Animal spiral stencil

Magic Glow Slate

Abracadabra and alakazam, write without a pencil, erase without an eraser. You can write notes and erase the evidence right away. This slate even glows in the dark! It's magic!

Directions:	Read and follow the instructions on pages 2-8. Print your request neatly on paper and put it in an envelope. You must enclose a 6x9 self-addressed stamped envelope and $1.00.
Write to:	Alvin Peters Company Dept. KP 2052-FK P.O. Box 2050 Albany, NY 12220-0050
Ask for:	Magic pink glow slate

Play-Doh

Play with Play-Doh. Create animals, buildings, balls, or whatever else you want to with your very own sample tub of Play-Doh. Just don't eat it!

Directions:	Read and follow the instructions on pages 2-8. Print your request neatly on paper and put it in an envelope. You must enclose a 6x9 self-addressed stamped envelope and 75¢.
Write to:	Alvin Peters Company Dept. 9832-FK P.O. Box 2050 Albany, NY 12220-0050
Ask for:	Play-Doh sample tub

Sun Catchers

Catch a ray of summer sun with these sun catchers! They look like stained glass and they are so cute you'll want to put them on every window in your house. You'll receive a dog, a teddy bear, or even a circus clown. Let the sun shine in! Be sure to specify which one you want.

Pirate Yo-Yo

Ahoy, matey! You can do all sorts of tricks with this scary pirate yo-yo. Keep it with you at all times to show off your yo-yo magic and to frighten away other pirates. It's a treasure!

Directions:	Read and follow the instructions on pages 2-8. **Print** your request **neatly** on paper and put it in an envelope. You must enclose **four 33¢ stamps** and **$1.00/ item.**
Write to:	RNM P.O. Box 542 FS Bethpage, NY 11714
Ask for:	Sun catchers

Directions:	Read and follow the instructions on pages 2-8. **Print** your request **neatly** on paper and put it in an envelope. You must enclose a **long self-addressed stamped envelope** and **50¢.**
Write to:	S.A.F.E. P.O. Box 40 1594 Brooklyn, NY 11240-1594
Ask for:	Scary pirate yo-yo

Mini Padlock

Not even the best robber could get into your backpack if you use this padlock. Its small size is perfect for a backpack or purse, and only you have the keys.

Directions:	**Read and follow the instructions on pages 2-8. Print** your request **neatly** on paper and put it in an envelope. You must enclose a **long self-addressed stamped envelope** and **$1.00.**
Write to:	Daisy Enterprises Dept. MPL P.O. Box 1426 Rutherfordton, NC 28139
Ask for:	Mini padlock

3D Magic Cards

When you look at these cards they just look like a lot of spots, but when you look closer you'll see that there are pictures inside. They're magnificently magical.

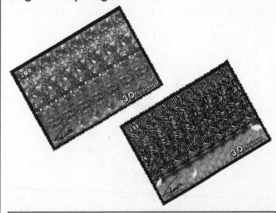

Directions:	**Read and follow the instructions on pages 2-8. Print** your request **neatly** on paper and put it in an envelope. You must enclose a **long self-addressed stamped envelope** and **50¢.**
Write to:	Kids' Shopper Magic 3D Card Offer 1822 Adams Missouri City, TX 77489
Ask for:	Two Magic 3D Cards

Chinese Checkers

Check it out! This magnetic Chinese checkers game can be played in the car without losing the pieces. It's small enough to fit in your back pocket or school bag, too, so you can play checkers whenever the mood checks out.

Directions:	Read and follow the instructions on pages 2-8. **Print** your request **neatly** on paper and put it in an envelope. You must enclose a **long self-addressed stamped envelope** and **$1.00.**
Write to:	The Surprise Gift of the Month Club P.O. Box 1-CC Stony Point, NY 10980
Ask for:	Magnetic chinese checkers

Checkers

You'll be seeing red and black with this pocket-sized checker game. This is a perfect game for traveling because it's small enough to bring anywhere.

Directions:	Read and follow the instructions on pages 2-8. **Print** your request **neatly** on paper and put it in an envelope. You must enclose a **long self-addressed stamped envelope** and **50¢.**
Write to:	The Kids' Shopper Checker Offer 1822 Adams Missouri City, TX 77489
Ask for:	Checkers

Old Maid

This old maid is a nice old lady. This old maid travel deck is a colorful and exciting game to play with another person or a whole group of friends.

astronaut

deep sea diver

old maid

Directions:	Read and follow the instructions on pages 2-8. **Print** your request **neatly** on paper and put it in an envelope. You must enclose a **long self-addressed stamped envelope** and **$1.00**.
Write to:	The Surprise Gift of the Month Club P.O. Box 1 - MC Stony Point, NY 10980
Ask for:	Old maid card game

Sticker Puzzle

It's puzzling—this sheet of stickers doesn't look like a puzzle, but it is! Now you can have the fun of a puzzle without keeping track of all the pieces. Each puzzle features a different Muppet character.

Directions:	Read and follow the instructions on pages 2-8. **Print** your request **neatly** on paper and put it in an envelope. You must enclose a **6x9 self-addressed stamped envelope** and **$1.00**.
Write to:	Alvin Peters Company Dept. MUFF77-FK P.O. Box 2050 Albany, NY 12220-0050
Ask for:	Muppets jumbled stickers

Fly a Kite

Go fly a kite! This kite is sure to be a hit at the beach or a picnic. Look up in the sky. It's a bird! It's a plane! No, it's your new kite!

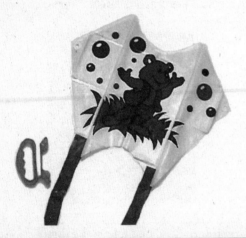

Directions:	Read and follow the instructions on pages 2-8. Print your request neatly on paper and put it in an envelope. You must enclose a long self-addressed stamped envelope and $1.00.
Write to:	The Surprise Gift of the Month Club P.O. Box 1 Stony Point, NY 10980
Ask for:	Kite

Beach Ball Fun

Be a beach bum with this beach ball. All the surfer dudes and dudettes will envy you when you start battin' around your new beach ball. Just keep it away from the sharks!

Directions:	Read and follow the instructions on pages 2-8. Print your request neatly on paper and put it in an envelope. You must enclose a long self-addressed stamped envelope and $1.00.
Write to:	The Kids' Shopper Beach Ball Offer 1822 Adams Missouri City, TX 77489
Ask for:	Beach ball

Reading

Assorted Cute Book Clips

These clips are a cute way to save your place in a book. Choose between an alligator, clown, or penguin. This is a fun and unique way to take a break from reading your books.

Directions:	Read and follow the instructions on pages 2-8. Print your request neatly on paper and put it in an envelope. You must enclose a **long self-addressed stamped envelope** and **50¢**.
Write to:	Edinboro Creations, Dept. BC 1210 Brierly Lane Munhall, PA 15120
Ask for:	Assorted cute book clips

Touch Me! Bookmark

Have you ever seen an animal change colors? When you rub these bookmarks, they turn into a rainbow of colors. You will receive a dolphin, monkey, or alligator. These are sure to amaze your friends and teachers.

Directions:	Read and follow the instructions on pages 2-8. Print your request neatly on paper and put it in an envelope. You must enclose a **long self-addressed stamped envelope** and **$1.00**.
Write to:	Edinboro Creations, Dept. BM 1210 Brierly Lane Munhall, PA 15120
Ask for:	Touch Me! bookmark

BOOKMARKS

Girls to the Rescue

Now here's a new idea! In all of these books, the girls are the heroes. They aren't waiting for Prince Charming to come and help—instead they just may be saving him! Send for this bookmark to find out about the first four books in this exciting series.

Directions:	Read and follow the instructions on pages 2-8. Print your request neatly on paper and put it in an envelope. You must enclose a long self-addressed stamped envelope.
Write to:	Meadowbrook Press 5451 Smetana Drive Minnetonka, MN 55343
Ask for:	Girls to the Rescue bookmark

Poetry Party

You may become addicted to poetry after you read one of the funny poetry books by Bruce Lansky. This bookmark will tell you about his six different books while the poems on the back are guaranteed to give you *A Bad Case of the Giggles*.

Directions:	Read and follow the instructions on pages 2-8. Print your request neatly on paper and put it in an envelope. You must enclose a long self-addressed stamped envelope.
Write to:	Meadowbrook Press 5451 Smetana Drive Minnetonka, MN 55343
Ask for:	Poetry Party bookmark

Money Bookmarks

Be worth a million dollars with these bookmarks that look like real money. You'll receive a $100 bill and a $50 bill. Just don't try to spend them!

Directions:	Read and follow the instructions on pages 2-8. Print your request neatly on paper and put it in an envelope. You must enclose a long self-addressed stamped envelope and 75¢.
Write to:	Neetstuff P.O. Box 353 Department FS-67 Rio Grande, NJ 08242
Ask for:	Laminated dollar bookmarks

Rainforest Bookmarks

Learn about the animals who live in the rainforest with these bookmarks. Each bookmark features a different animal like the chameleon, sloth, toucan, ocelot, or leafcutting ants on the front and information about the animal on the back. You can either receive one for 25¢ or five for $1.00.

Chameleon

Directions:	Read and follow the instructions on pages 2-8. Print your request neatly on paper and put it in an envelope. You must enclose a long self-addressed stamped envelope and 25¢ for one, or a long self-addressed stamped envelope and $1.00 for five.
Write to:	Daisy Enterprises Dept. RFAB P.O Box 1426 Rutherfordton, NC 28139
Ask for:	Rain forest animal bookmark(s)

No More Homework! No More Tests!

No more homework! No more tests! Your teacher may not agree but you can always try! Let your teacher and classmates know how you feel by wearing one of these cool buttons. Tell your friends to wear one too and see if it works!

Directions:	Read and follow the instructions on pages 2-8. Print your request neatly on paper and put it in an envelope. You must enclose a long self-addressed stamped envelope and 50¢.
Write to:	Meadowbrook Press 5451 Smetana Drive Minnetonka, MN 55343
Ask for:	No More Homework! No More Tests! button

Mini Book Binding Kit

Make your own mini book with cover, pages, and authentic binding. You will receive all the illustrated instructions and materials you need to make a mini book. Perfect for a journal, address book, or gift!

Directions:	Read and follow the instructions on pages 2-8. Print your request neatly on paper and put it in an envelope. You must enclose $1.00.
Write to:	Alaska Craft Box 11-1102 Anchorage, AK 99511-1102
Ask for:	Mini book binding kit

ACTIVITY MAGAZINES

Science Weekly

Put a little science in your week with a free sample issue of *Science Weekly*, a magazine just for kids in grades K–8. Learn about all sorts of exciting things!

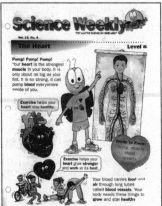

Directions:	**Read and follow the instructions on pages 2-8. Print** your request **neatly** on paper and put it in an envelope. You must enclose a **long self-addressed stamped envelope.**
Write to:	Stock-Vaughn Co. Attn: Science Weekly P.O. Box 26015 Austin, TX 78755
Ask for:	Science Weekly sample issue

Art and History Coloring Books

Color your way to exciting times in history! Be a coloring book artist! Have fun learning about history with this educational pamphlet that features an excellent choice of books to order.

Directions:	**Read and follow the instructions on pages 2-8. Print** your request **neatly** on paper and put it in an envelope. You must enclose a **long self-addressed stamped envelope** with a **76¢ stamp.**
Write to:	Bellerophon Books P.O. Box 21307 Santa Barbara, CA 93121
Ask for:	Art and history coloring books

Sprocket Man

It's not a bird or a plane—it's Sprocket Man! This coloring book will tell you everything you need to know about being a safe and careful biker. Biking should be a safe and fun sport, and Sprocket Man will teach you how to be a superhero on bike safety, too.

Directions:	Read and follow the instructions on pages 2-8. **Print** your request **neatly** on paper and put it in an envelope. You must enclose a **long self-addressed stamped envelope.**
Write to:	U. S. Consumer Product Safety Commission Washington, DC 20207
Ask for:	Sprocket Man coloring book

Money Comic Books

Money for free? Not quite! But you can read all about the history of money—from bartering to the present-day banking system—in these exciting comic books. Now that's a good deal!

Directions:	Read and follow the instructions on pages 2-8. **Print** your request **neatly** on paper and put it in an envelope.
Write to:	Federal Reserve Bank of New York 33 Liberty Street New York, NY 10045
Ask for:	Federal Reserve comic books

Horsepower Magazine

Do you love horses? If so, this magazine is perfect for you. *Horsepower* is a magazine for young horse lovers, with stories, games, and fun features like your horse-scopes. Learning about your horse has never been so fun.

Directions:	**Read and follow the instructions on pages 2-8. Print** your request **neatly** on paper and put it in an envelope. You must enclose a **long self-addressed stamped envelope and 50¢.**
Write to:	Horsepower Magazine P.O. Box 670 Aurora, ON Canada L4G 4J9
Ask for:	Horsepower magazine

Personalized Book

Wouldn't it be fun to be the star of your own book? You can be. This pamphlet will tell you how to order your own personalized book. You will also receive a $2.00-off coupon on ordering your first book.

Directions:	**Read and follow the instructions on pages 2-8. Print** your request **neatly** on paper and put it in an envelope. You must enclose a **long self-addressed stamped envelope.**
Write to:	Daisy Enterprises Dept. Book P.O. Box 1426 Rutherfordton, NC 28139
Ask for:	Personalized book info and $2.00 off coupon

Animal Rights Magazine

Grrr! This 'zine will bite you with interesting stories about animals and animal rights. You'll receive a free issue of the magazine, and you can decide if you want to order a subscription. Learn about how you can make a difference in the lives of animals.

Directions:	Read and follow the instructions on pages 2-8. Print your request neatly on paper and put it in an envelope.
Write to:	PETA Education Department 501 Front Street Norfolk, VA 23510
Ask for:	GRRR! magazine

Pack-O-Fun Magazine

This magazine really is a Pack-O-Fun! Filled with creative projects and fun stuff for kids to do, this magazine is guaranteed to keep your hands busy. You'll also receive a free project sheet. Receive a trial issue and decide if you want to subscribe at a discounted rate, or cancel your subscription right away with no obligation.

Directions:	Read and follow the instructions on pages 2-8. Print your request neatly on paper and put it in an envelope.
Write to:	Clapper Publishing Co., Inc. 2400 East Devon, #375 Des Plaines, IL 60018
Ask for:	Pack-O- Fun F014PFS1

Poetic License

Do you want to be a poet? Then send for this poetic license. You can impress your classmates and teachers with this proof of your poetic soul. Just be sure to carry it with you at all times!

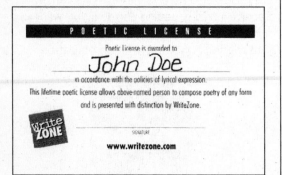

Creative with Words

A magazine that publishes stories written by kids? That's right! You can be a published writer. Send for the guidelines and instructions and learn how you can become the world's most famous writer. Well, maybe not right away, but this is a great place to start!

Directions:	**Read and follow the instructions on pages 2-8. Print** your request **neatly** on paper and put it in an envelope. You must enclose a **long self-addressed stamped envelope.**
Write to:	WriteZone 8019 SW 35th Avenue, #5 Portland, OR 97219
Ask for:	Poetic license

Directions:	**Read and follow the instructions on pages 2-8. Print** your request **neatly** on paper and put it in an envelope. You must enclose a **long self-addressed stamped envelope.**
Write to:	Creative with Words Publications P.O. Box 223226 Carmel, CA 93922
Ask for:	Creative with Words publications

ENVIRONMENT

KIND News

Learn how to be KIND to nature by reading this newsletter. KIND news has interesting stories about animals, the environment, and even movie stars! Kids can make a difference! Be sure to specify your grade level because there are different newspapers for different ages.

Carly's Jr. Steward

The rain forest covers only 2 percent of the earth's surface, but it is home to over half the plants and animals in the world. Find out what you can do to help the rainforest. It needs you!

Directions:	Read and follow the instructions on pages 2-8. **Print** your request **neatly** on paper and put it in an envelope. You must enclose a **long self-addressed stamped envelope**.
Write to:	NAHEE/ KIND News (FSK) P.O. Box 362 East Haddam, CT 06423-0362
Ask for:	KIND News newspaper (specify your grade level)

Directions:	Read and follow the instructions on pages 2-8. **Print** your request **neatly** on paper and put it in an envelope.
Write to:	National Arbor Day Foundation 211 N. 12th, Ste. 501 Lincoln, NE 68508
Ask for:	Carly's Junior Steward

Ranger Rick

You'll love this issue of *Ranger Rick* that features frogs and funny noses in nature. Receive this issue or another exciting one and decide if you want to subscribe. For ages 7-12, *Ranger Rick* is full of amazing animal facts, photos, games, puzzles, and other fun activities.

Directions:	Read and follow the instructions on pages 2-8. **Print** your request **neatly** on paper and put it in an envelope.
Write to:	National Wildlife Federation Attn: Publications 8925 Leesburg Pike Vienna, VA 22184
Ask for:	Ranger Rick

Save the Manatee

Be the only kid on your block to adopt a manatee. Of course, you can't actually bring this one thousand pound mammal home because it needs to stay in its natural habitat. Manatees are an endangered species and need to be protected. Find out what you can do to help.

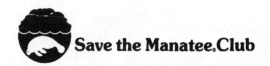

Save the Manatee.Club

Directions:	Read and follow the instructions on pages 2-8. **Print** your request **neatly** on paper and put it in an envelope. You must enclose a **long self-addressed stamped envelope** with **a 55¢ stamp**.
Write to:	Save the Manatee Club 500 N. Maitland Avenue Maitland, FL 34787
Ask for:	Manatee student education packet (specify your grade level)

Pen Pals

Make friends with other kids across the nation who care about protecting animals and nature. You will receive an application to register for free in ARK's Animalkind Kids Worldwide humane education program, a member ID card, info on how to receive letters from pen pals, and a pet owner's checklist brochure.

Directions:	Read and follow the instructions on pages 2-8. **Print** your request **neatly** on paper and put it in an envelope. You must enclose a **long self-addressed stamped envelope.**
Write to:	A.R.K.—Animalkind Rescue Kids P.O. Box 1271 San Luis Obispo, CA 93406
Ask for:	Pen pal registration

Cut Out Dissection

Cutting up frogs, cats, worms, and other animals is disgusting. Ewww! But cutting them up—dissecting—is done all the time in classrooms. Learn other alternatives to this cruel process and do yourself and these animals a favor. Standing up for your beliefs isn't always easy, but it's always cool!

Directions:	Read and follow the instructions on pages 2-8. **Print** your request **neatly** on paper and put it in an envelope.
Write to:	NAVS Dissection Hotline 53 W. Jackson Blvd Ste. 1552 Chicago, IL 60604
Ask for:	Say No to Dissection handbook

Awesome Offer

Growing Alligator

What is slimy, green, and grows five to six times bigger than its original size in water? Your very own growing alligator! You'll shed crocodile tears when you see how big this alligator actually grows! Also, did you know that crocodiles are the closest living relatives to dinosaurs?

Directions:	Read and follow the instructions on pages 2-8. Print your request neatly on paper and put it in an envelope. You must enclose a long self-addressed stamped envelope and $1.00.
Write to:	Phil Labush 9360 Northwest 39th Street Sunrise, FL 33351
Ask for:	Growing alligator

Bug Bracelet Kit

If you have entomophobia, a fear of bugs, this offer may be a little scary. These creepy, crawly bugs love hanging around your wrist and on your keys, and they glow in the dark! Everything is included in the kit. You may select either two bracelets, two key chains, or one bracelet and one key chain.

Directions:	Read and follow the instructions on pages 2-8. Print your request neatly on paper and put it in an envelope. You must enclose a long self-addressed stamped envelope and 75¢.
Write to:	A.R.K.—Animalkind Rescue Kids It's a Bug's Life P.O. Box 1271 San Luis Obispo, CA 93406
Ask for:	It's a Bug's Life glow-in-the-dark bracelet and key chain kit

Sticky Butterfly

This butterfly doesn't just fly, it swings! Swing your butterfly by the tail and watch it stick on glass, mirrors, or paper. The tail stretches up to five feet. If you like butterflies, you'll love this offer.

Directions:	Read and follow the instructions on pages 2-8. **Print** your request **neatly** on paper and put it in an envelope. You must enclose a **long self-addressed stamped envelope** and **50¢.**
Write to:	Daisy Enterprises Dept. STUL P.O. Box 1426 Rutherfordton, NC 28139
Ask for:	Sticky butterfly

Suction Reptile

This reptile loves to hang around. It has suction cups on its belly so you can stick it on mirrors or windows. It's green and it's sticky—what more could you want?

Directions:	Read and follow the instructions on pages 2-8. **Print** your request **neatly** on paper and put it in an envelope. You must enclose a **long self-addressed stamped envelope** and **50¢.**
Write to:	Daisy Enterprises Dept. SRT P.O. Box 1426 Rutherfordton, NC 28139
Ask for:	Suction reptile

Bumper Sticker

Go and hug a tree! Let everyone know how much you care about trees by putting this bumper sticker on your parents' car, your bike, or anywhere else. Let there be trees!

Trees for Life

Plant love all over the world! Get all of your friends to wear one of these buttons and make a difference in the future of our trees. You will receive four buttons.

Directions:	Read and follow the instructions on pages 2-8. **Print** your request **neatly** on paper and put it in an envelope. You must enclose a **long self-addressed stamped envelope** and **$1.00**.
Write to:	Trees for Life 3006 W. St. Louis Wichita, KS 67203-5129
Ask for:	Bumper sticker

Directions:	Read and follow the instructions on pages 2-8. **Print** your request **neatly** on paper and put it in an envelope. You must enclose a **long self-addressed stamped envelope** and **$1.00**.
Write to:	Trees for Life 3006 W. St. Louis Wichita, KS 67203-5129
Ask for:	Tree buttons

Save the Planet

Help the rainforest and our earth stick around with these stickers. The planet is in a sticky situation, and you can recognize this by sticking these stickers where everyone can see them. Request either Save the Rainforest or Help Protect Your Earth stickers.

Metallic Earth Stickers

You've heard of mother earth, but have you ever heard of sleeping earth, skateboarding earth, dancing earth, or relaxing earth? Probably not, but then you haven't seen these stickers. They even have a groovy metallic sheen!

Directions:	Read and follow the instructions on pages 2-8. **Print** your request **neatly** on paper and put it in an envelope. You must enclose a **long self-addressed stamped envelope** and **35¢.**
Write to:	S.A.F.E. P.O. Box 40 1594 Brooklyn, NY 11240-1594
Ask for:	Help Protect Your Earth **or** Save the Rainforest stickers

Directions:	Read and follow the instructions on pages 2-8. **Print** your request **neatly** on paper and put it in an envelope. You must enclose a **long self-addressed stamped envelope** and **75¢.**
Write to:	Alvin Peters Company Dept. 99 OES P.O. Box 2050 Albany, NY 12220-0050
Ask for:	Our Earth stickers

Animal Awareness Pack

Are you aware of your animals? If you are a pet owner, you should be. This package contains four color-me postcards, animal erasers, and a glow-in-the-dark paw print ring.

PLEASE Spay and Neuter US!

Directions:	Read and follow the instructions on pages 2-8. **Print** your request **neatly** on paper and put it in an envelope. You must enclose a **long self-addressed stamped envelope and 75¢.**
Write to:	P.A.L.S. Animal Awareness Pack P.O. Box 1271 San Luis Obispo, CA 93406
Ask for:	Animal awareness pack

Recycling Awareness

Reduce, reuse, recycle. Keep your street clean and make a difference with these recycling projects. Involve your neighborhood or school, too!

Recycling Rover

Directions:	Read and follow the instructions on pages 2-8. **Print** your request **neatly** on paper and put it in an envelope. You must enclose a **long self-addressed stamped envelope and 25¢.**
Write to:	P.A.L.S. Recycling Awareness P.O. Box 1271 San Luis Obispo, CA 93406
Ask for:	Recycling awareness

Magic Seeds

Jack in the Beanstalk was just a fairy tale, but with these magical seeds, you can grow an amazing bean pole, too. Or you can grow sunflowers taller than your house. Just plant, water, and wait for the magic to begin.

Directions:	Read and follow the instructions on pages 2-8. Print your request neatly on paper and put it in an envelope. You must enclose a long self-addressed stamped envelope and $1.00.
Write to:	S & D Dept. H P.O. Box 114 Casey, IL 62420
Ask for:	Bean and sunflower seeds

Flower Power

Grow a garden to rival your grandma's with these flower seeds. Go crazy with daisies, create delirium with nasturtiums, win and grin with zinnias! You'll have a rainbow in your own backyard. You'll receive five packs.

Directions:	Read and follow the instructions on pages 2-8. Print your request neatly on paper and put it in an envelope. You must enclose a long self-addressed stamped envelope and $1.00.
Write to:	Surprise Gift of the Month Club P.O. Box 1- MS Stony Point, NY 10980
Ask for:	Flower seeds

MEADOWBROOK PRESS

2000 EDITION

U.S. MAIL

AWARENESS AND SELF-ESTEEM

911

Make the right call in an emergency—call 911. Hang this poster by the phone so you know what to dial if you are ever in an emergency.

Bike Safety

Use your head when riding a bike: first, by being safe and smart, and second, by wearing a bicycle helmet. This poster is a cool reminder to be bike safe!

Directions:	Read and follow the instructions on pages 2-8. Print your request neatly on paper and put it in an envelope.
Write to:	FEMA P.O. Box 2012 Jessup, MD 20794
Ask for:	Make the Right Call (911) poster

Directions:	Read and follow the instructions on pages 2-8. Print your request neatly on paper and put it in an envelope.
Write to:	U. S. Consumer Product Safety Commission Washington, DC 20207
Ask for:	Bike safety poster

Get M.A.D.D.

Go M.A.D.D. with this great offer. Learn about the dangers of drinking and driving by doing puzzles, playing games, and reading awesome stories about your favorite celebrities. Be sure to specify your age because there are different activities for different age groups.

Mothers Against Drunk Driving

Fight against Crime

Take a bite out of crime with McGruff, the safety dog. Halloween safety is just one of the cool things you can learn about. You can also request an identification kit where you can record your very own completely unique fingerprints.

Directions:	Read and follow the instructions on pages 2-8. Print your request neatly on paper and put it in an envelope.
Write to:	M.A.D.D. 511 W. John Carpenter Freeway Suite 700 Irving, TX 75062
Ask for:	M.A.D.D. publication (specify age)

Directions:	Read and follow the instructions on pages 2-8. Print your request neatly on paper and put it in an envelope. You must enclose a long long self-addressed stamped envelope with two stamps and $1.00.
Write to:	Boerner, Inc McGruff Safety Kids 15500 Wayzata Blvd., #1007 Wayzata, MN 55391
Ask for:	McGruff safety kit

Fire Safety

Fire is a leading cause of accidental death in the home each year in the United States. Help your family be fire safe. Now that's a hot idea!

Family Disaster Plan

Where will your family be when disaster strikes? Prepare a plan with your family in advance. Families can—and do—cope with disaster every day. Be prepared.

Directions:	**Read and follow the instructions on pages 2-8. Print** your request **neatly** on paper and put it in an envelope.
Write to:	U. S. Consumer Product Safety Commission Washington, DC 20207
Ask for:	Fire safety information

Directions:	**Read and follow the instructions on pages 2-8. Print** your request **neatly** on paper and put it in an envelope.
Write to:	FEMA P.O. Box 2012 Jessup, MD 20794
Ask for:	Family Disaster Plan pamphlet

Breathe Easy

You'll breathe with ease if you say no to cigarettes! You have only one pair of lungs, so keep them clean and healthy! Request either a No Smoking activity book or a Healthy Lungs poster.

Directions:	Read and follow the instructions on pages 2-8. **Print** your request **neatly** on paper and put it in an envelope.
Write to:	American Lung Association G.P.O. Box 596 New York, NY 10116-0596
Ask for:	Activity book or Healthy Lungs poster

Cruelty-Free Shopping

Be a cruelty-free shopper and choose companies that don't test their products on animals. You'll be a caring consumer and a good friend to rabbits, mice, and monkeys.

Directions:	Read and follow the instructions on pages 2-8. **Print** your request **neatly** on paper and put it in an envelope.
Write to:	PETA Education Department 501 Front Street Norfolk, VA 23510
Ask for:	Caring Consumer Cruelty-Free Shopping Guide

Magnetic Magic

This pyramid isn't in Egypt, it should be on your refrigerator! Getting the right daily food choices will make you strong and healthy. Unfortunately, chocolate isn't one of those choices! You can also request a "Bone Up on Calcium" magnet instead of the food guide.

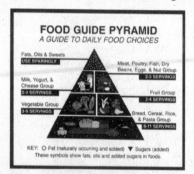

Directions:	**Read and follow the instructions on pages 2-8. Print** your request **neatly** on paper and put it in an envelope. You must enclose a **long self-addressed stamped envelope** and **$1.00**.
Write to:	Learning Zone Express Box 1022 Owatanna, MN 55060
Ask for:	Food Guide Pyramid or Bone Up on Calcium magnet

Magnet Frames

Freeze frame your fabulous face—or the fantastic faces of your friends or family—with this metallic, magnetic picture frame. Your frames will be fab!

Directions:	**Read and follow the instructions on pages 2-8. Print** your request **neatly** on paper and put it in an envelope. You must enclose **$1.00**
Write to:	Hicks Specialties 1308 68th Lane N. Brooklyn Center, MN 55430
Ask for:	Magnetic fridge frames

Self-Esteem Stickers

Isn't it great that you're you and nobody else? These stickers are a wonderful celebration of you being you. Put these stickers on your notebook, or give them to your friends, and be happy about being 100 percent unique!

Directions:	Read and follow the instructions on pages 2-8. Print your request neatly on paper and put it in an envelope. You must enclose a long self-addressed stamped envelope and 45¢.
Write to:	S.A.F.E. P.O. Box 40 1594 Brooklyn, NY 11240-1594
Ask for:	Self-esteem stickers

ABC Feelings

Now I've learned my ABCs, next time won't you play with me! Remember that rhyme? Now you can have a full color postcard that has a whole alphabet of words describing how you feel. Or, you can send this postcard to a good friend and let them know just how special they are!

Directions:	Read and follow the instructions on pages 2-8. Print your request neatly on paper and put it in an envelope. You must enclose a long self-addressed stamped envelope and 50¢.
Write to:	ABC Feelings Inc. P.O. Box 2377 Coeur d'Alene, ID 83816-2377
Ask for:	ABC Feelings postcard

Birthday Letter

Do you know what else happened on the day you were born? What were the famous movies and songs? What famous people do you share your birthday with? All these questions can be answered with this calendar page of the most important day ever, your birthday! Include your first name, last name, and birthdate.

Birthday

Newsletter

Directions:	Read and follow the instructions on pages 2-8. **Print** your request **neatly** on paper and put it in an envelope. You must enclose a **long self-addressed stamped envelope and $1.00**.
Write to:	Daisy Enterprises Dept. News P.O. Box 1426 Rutherfordton, NC 28139
Ask for:	Birthday newsletter

Celebrity Addresses

Would you like to write to your favorite star and tell them how much you like them? Maybe even ask for an autographed picture? Drew Barrymore, Leonardo DiCaprio, and Kate Winslet are just a few of the stars you can write to. Receive information on how to find the stars for free, or send $1.00 and let someone else find up to three addresses for you. Stars' names must be listed if addresses are requested.

 ADDRESSES of the STARS!*

Directions:	Read and follow the instructions on pages 2-8. **Print** your request **neatly** on paper and put it in an envelope. You must enclose a **long self-addressed stamped envelope** for information on getting celebrity addresses and a **long self-addressed stamped envelope** and **$1.00** to have the addresses found for you.
Write to:	Daisy Enterprises Dept. Stars or Star Info P.O. Box 1426 Rutherfordton, NC 28139
Ask for:	Celebrity addresses

I Have a Dream

Dr. Martin Luther King, Jr., said, "I have a dream that children will one day live in a nation where they will not be judged by the color of their skin but by the content of their character." This bookmark is a wonderful reminder of these words.

Directions:	Read and follow the instructions on pages 2-8. Print your request neatly on paper and put it in an envelope. You must enclose a long self-addressed stamped envelope and 25¢.
Write to:	Daisy Enterprises Dept. MLK P.O. Box 1426 Rutherfordton, NC 28139
Ask for:	"I Have a Dream" bookmark

Animal Combs

Comb your hair with a dog! What? No, not a real dog—Fido probably wouldn't appreciate that. But with these animal combs you can look good and love animals at the same time! You'll receive either a dog, whale, sea horse, or walrus.

Directions:	Read and follow the instructions on pages 2-8. Print your request neatly on paper and put it in an envelope. You must enclose a long envelope and 50¢.
Write to:	Edinboro Creations Dept. COMB 1210 Brierly Lane Munhall, PA 15120
Ask for:	Cute animal combs

Friendship Pins

Give your friends a pin to show them you care. Each colored bead has a different meaning, like, "You're Nice!" "Best Friends!" or "I Love You!" Friends are forever, so give them a friendship pin to show them you care!

Friend Purses

Keep your money in these purses. They are the perfect size for your pocket or even to put on your keychain. The colorful smiley faces and flowers are sure to let everyone know that you are a friend!

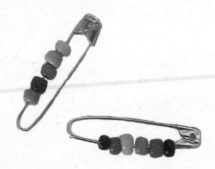

Directions:	Read and follow the instructions on pages 2-8. Print your request neatly on paper and put it in an envelope. You must enclose a long self-addressed stamped envelope and 75¢.
Write to:	Daisy Enterprises Dept. FP P.O. Box 1426 Rutherfordton, NC 28139
Ask for:	Friendship pins

Directions:	Read and follow the instructions on pages 2-8. Print your request neatly on paper and put it in an envelope. You must enclose a long self-addressed stamped envelope and 75¢.
Write to:	Phil Labush 9360 Northwest 39th Street Sunrise, FL 33351
Ask for:	Friends See Through Purse

WORLD CULTURE

Foreign Nature Stamps

Animals are different all over the world. See some of the unique animals in foreign countries on these stamps that are an excellent addition to any collection. You will receive twenty-five different cancelled foreign stamps.

United Nations

These stamps may be old but are actually still usable. The United Nations makes sure that the countries of the world work together. Learn about the U.N. and get some of their hard-to-find stamps.

Directions:	**Read and follow the instructions on pages 2-8. Print** your request **neatly** on paper and put it in an envelope. You must enclose a **long self-addressed stamped envelope** and **$1.00.** *Cash or postal money order only.*
Write to:	Universal P.O. Box 466 Port Washington, NY 11050
Ask for:	Nature stamps

Directions:	**Read and follow the instructions on pages 2-8. Print** your request **neatly** on paper and put it in an enve-lope. You must enclose a **long self-addressed stamped envelope** and **$1.00.** *Cash or postal money order only.*
Write to:	J. Alexander P.O. Box 7-Dept. UN Roslyn, NY 11576
Ask for:	United Nations stamps

Foreign Coins

Money is different all over the world. While the USA puts presidents on our money, the coins from other countries shows nature scenes, writers, and even fish! You'll receive five different coins from Surinam, Hungary, Iceland, Poland, and Yugoslavia.

Foreign Bills

What do kids in Lithuania or Croatia buy fun things with? See what paper money looks like in five of the newer nations formed from the break up of the communist world. You will receive bank notes form Lithuania, Croatia, Ukraine, Belarus, and Macedonia.

Directions:	Read and follow the instructions on pages 2-8. Print your request neatly on paper and put it in an envelope. You must enclose a long self-addressed stamped envelope and $1.00. No personal checks.
Write to:	Jolie Coins P.O. Box 68 - Dept. MC Roslyn Heights, NY 11577-0068
Ask for:	Foreign coins

Directions:	Read and follow the instructions on pages 2-8. Print your request neatly on paper and put it in an envelope. You must enclose a long self-addressed stamped envelope and $1.00. No personal checks.
Write to:	Jolie Coins P.O. Box 68 - Dept. MN Roslyn Heights, NY 11577-0068
Ask for:	Foreign banknotes

Festival Money

Chinese festival money is used all over Asia for different celebrations. It's not real money, but it's what kids use during their New Years, Bright Moon, and Ghost Day Festival (like our Halloween). Plus, you will receive information and history about the money.

Chinese Finger Trap

This is a great (and safe) trick to play on your friends. This finger trap traps the fingers so that it is difficult to get them free. Perfect for sticky fingers!

Directions:	Read and follow the instructions on pages 2-8. Print your request neatly on paper and put it in an envelope. You must enclose a long self-addressed stamped envelope and 25¢.
Write to:	Chinese Festival Money 3600 Whitney Avenue Sacramento, CA 95821-3128
Ask for:	Chinese festival money

Directions:	Read and follow the instructions on pages 2-8. Print your request neatly on paper and put it in an envelope. You must enclose a long self-addressed stamped envelope and 50¢.
Write to:	The Kids Shopper Finger Trap Offer 1822 Adams Missouri City, TX 77489
Ask for:	Chinese fingertrap

World Pen Pals

Find a pen pal from the other side of the world. You will receive an application to meet a friend from any continent except Australia. Say *ça va* or *cómo estás* to your new friend across the ocean!

WORLD PEN PALS
P.O. Box 337
Saugerties, NY 12477 USA

Directions:	Read and follow the instructions on pages 2-8. **Print** your request **neatly** on paper and put it in an envelope. You must enclose a **long self-addressed stamped envelope** and **25¢.**
Write to:	World Pen Pals P.O. Box 337 Saugerties, NY 12477
Ask for:	World Pen Pal application

Save a Life

You could save a life by writing a letter. Get involved with Amnesty International and help people all over the world who are imprisoned, hurt, or even worse. You will receive the Children's Edition Urgent Action pack, which includes stickers, info on kids in danger, games, and instructions on how to write a letter that really could save a life.

Directions:	Read and follow the instructions on pages 2-8. **Print** your request **neatly** on paper and put it in an envelope.
Write to:	Amnesty International USA Children's Edition Urgent Action P.O. Box 1270 Nederland, CO 80466-1270
Ask for:	Children's Edition UA pack

SEE THE WORLD

To receive free tourist information on foreign countries, send a postcard with your name, address, and request to the following addresses.

Austria
Austrian National Tourist Office
P.O. Box 1142
New York, NY 10108-1142

Aruba
Aruba Tourism Authority
1000 Harbor Blvd.
Weehawken, NJ 07087

Bahamas
Bahamas Tourist Office
150 E. 52nd Street
28th Floor North
New York, NY 10022

Belgium
Belgian Tourist Office
780 Third Avenue #1501
New York, NY 10017

China
China National Tourist Office
350 Fifth Avenue #6413
New York, NY 10118

Cote Dílvoire
Tourisme Cote Dílvoire
2424 Massachusetts Avenue NW
Washington, DC 20008

Egypt
Egyptian Tourist Authority
630 Fifth Avenue, #1706
New York, NY 10111

Fiji
Fiji Visitors Bureau
5777 W. Century Blvd. #220
Los Angeles, CA 90045

France
French Government Tourist Office
444 Madison Avenue
New York, NY 10022

Guatemala
Martinez Associates
2216 Coral Way
Miami, FL 33145

Indonesia
Indonesia Tourist Promotion Office
3457 Wilshire Boulevard
Los Angeles, CA 9001 0

Israel
Israel Government Tourist Office
800 Second Avenue
New York, NY 10017

Italy
Italian Government Travel Office
630 Fifth Avenue #1565
New York, NY 10111

Japan
Japan National Tourist Organization
One Rockefeller Plaza, #1250
New York, NY 10020

Kenya
Kenya Tourist Office
9150 Wilshire Boulevard #160
Beverly Hills, CA 90212

Mexico
Mexican Government Tourist
Office
405 Park Avenue #1401
New York, NY 10022

Nepal
Nepal Tourist Information
820 2nd Avenue #202
New York, NY 10017

New Zealand
New Zealand Tourism Board
501 Santa Monica Boulevard
#300
Santa Monica, CA 90401

Norway
Norwegian Tourist Board
655 Third Avenue #1810
New York, NY 10017

Philippines
Philippine Department of
Tourism
556 Fifth Avenue
New York, NY 10036

Portugal
Portuguese Trade and Tourism
Office
590 Fifth Avenue
New York, NY 10036-4704

Russian Federation
Russian National Tourist Office
800 3rd Avenue #3101
New York, NY 10022

Saint Lucia
St. Vincent and the Grenadines
Tourist Office
801 Second Avenue
21st Floor
New York, NY 10017

South Africa
South African Tourist Board
500 Fifth Avenue #2040
New York, NY 10110

Sweden
Swedish Travel and Tourism
Council
655 Third Avenue
New York, NY 10017

Tahiti
Tahiti Tourism Board
300 North Continental #180
El Segundo, CA 90245

Turkey
Turkish Tourist Office
1717 Massachusetts Avenue
NW #306
Washington, DC 20036

Uruguay
Uruguay Tourist Office
1077 Ponce de Leon Blvd.
Coral Gables, FL 33134

Zimbabwe
Zimbabwe Tourist Office
1270 Avenue of the Americas
New York, NY 10020

World Key Chain

This offer is truly out of this world! You'll receive a world key chain that's like a miniature globe. Now you can always know where in the world you are!

Directions:	**Read and follow the instructions on pages 2-8. Print** your request **neatly** on paper and put it in an envelope. You must enclose a **long self-addressed stamped envelope and 85¢.**
Write to:	S.A.F.E. P.O. Box 40 1594 Brooklyn, NY 11240-1594
Ask for:	Global key chain

Earth Coin Purse

Carry the world on your shoulders with this miniature earth coin purse. It's the perfect place to keep change, paper clips, erasers, and more! Plus, you can let everyone know just how much you love the earth!

Directions:	**Read and follow the instructions on pages 2-8. Print** your request **neatly** on paper and put it in an envelope. You must enclose a **long self-addressed stamped envelope and $1.00.**
Write to:	Daisy Enterprises Dept. ECP P.O. Box 1426 Rutherfordton, NC 28139
Ask for:	Earth coin purse

THE INTERNET

Free Stuff on the Internet

The Internet is the fastest growing form of communication today—it's also lots of fun. If you have access to a computer that's hooked up to the World Wide Web, you can use the addresses below and on the following pages to receive lots of fun and interesting stuff free!

Directions: First, you need access to a computer that is hooked up to the World Wide Web. A variety of online services provide Internet access. Find out which online server your computer uses and learn how to use that server. Then open the browser, type the URL address into the space provided, and hit return (or enter). Web addresses always begin with **http://** (which will help you know where to type).

Many of the sites listed on these pages allow you to download free software, including video games, screensavers, and other fun stuff. Here are the types of free software on the Internet:

Shareware—Games and other software that work for a limited amount of time or only contain a portion of the program. Shareware is meant to entice you into buying the full version of the game (although you don't have to).

Freeware—Full versions of games and other software for free! Sometimes old software is turned into freeware by companies to promote sequels.

Abandonware—Games and other software that are more than two years old and are no longer sold.

In addition, many sites feature games to play online. Sometimes these games are played against other human opponents online, and usually they require no downloads and can be played straight from your browser.

Good luck and happy surfing!

SOFTWARE

URL: http://www.kinderplanet.com
Shareware, freeware, and demos for children. This site also includes arts and crafts, games, music, and a book club.

URL: http://www.kidsdomain.com
Downloads, free contests, and treasure hunts are just a few of the fun things you'll find on this site.

GAMES

URL: http://www.cyberkids.com
An awesome site for cyberkids! Puzzles, stories, and games are just some of the cool free things on this site.

URL: http://www.bonus.com
This awesome musical site has free space games, coloring sites, and cool puzzles.

URL: http://www.kids-channel.co.uk
This England-based website has fun stories, information about children in need, and fun puzzle games.

URL: http://www.boowakwala.com
Play fun interactive games, read a great illustrated story, and listen to music and songs. This site is for children 2–8 years olds.

FUN STUFF FOR KIDS

URL: http://www.funschool.com
Fun activities for grades K–6. Each grade has different fun and educational activities, including contests to win a T-shirt and much, much more.

URL: http://www.freezone.com
Excellent chat room just for kids where you can chat with kids performing in Broadway shows, make new friends, and find out what other kids think about sports, pop culture, and more.

URL: http://scholastic.com/goosebumps
The Goosebumps web page is a ghoulishly fun page. Find out about the books, read stories, and more—that is, if you dare!

URL: http://worldkids.net
This out-of-this-world site is an imaginative journey into the Internet. Join a cast of characters including a dog, a hand puppet, and some cute little critters as you learn to surf the net.

URL: http://disney.go.com
Where the magic comes alive! Visit all your favorite Disney characters and play games, get your Disney horoscope, learn about new movies and music, and have a magical time!

URL: http://www.maxvikfunpage.com
Send a free cyber card, enjoy games, riddles, books, and even find a pen pal through this fun site organized by teachers.

URL: http://www.kidsloveamystery.com
If you love mysteries, you'll love this website. There are new mysteries to solve every week, and you can even join a Nancy Drew chat line to meet other kids who love mysteries.

URL: http://www.childrensmusic.org
This site is dedicated to music for children. Cool links, songs, and concert schedules are just some of the features of this site.

URL: http://www.bconnex.net/~kidworld
Enter a free writing contest, learn funny jokes, or ask for advice from Javi!

URL: http://www.kids-space.org:80
This space just for kids has music connections, international information for kids, and a link to a cool site from Japan!

URL: http://www.excite.com/games/kids
Play a Mr. Potato type game, listen to music, and get great free craft ideas.

URL: http://www.kidsurfer.org
Visit a virtual village, a virtual farm, and send a letter from a virtual post office on this site.

a gentle kiss,   a big sister lift,

a circle inviting you in . . .
or a peaceful rest!

Forever Wherever

by Sunny Dée
Art by Constanza Basaluzzo

I'll hug you goodbye,
I'll hug you hello,

I'll love you forever,
Wherever I go.

URL: http://www.gigglepoetry.com
If you love funny poetry, or if you want to write funny poetry, you'll love this site!

URL: http://www.randomhouse.com/Suessville
Dr. Suess has his very own site with cool graphics, activities, and fun.

EDUCATIONAL

URL: http://www.theideabox.com
This page is centered on fun ideas! Share your ideas with other kids, enter free contests and win prizes, or learn about late-breaking news for kids.

URL: http://www.kidsonline.com
Go on scavenger hunts, watch some virtual magic tricks, and learn how to make your own website.

URL: http://www.rollanet.org/kids
This website features coloring books, connections to cool, safe kids' sites, science projects, and much, much more!

URL: http://www.whitehouse.gov/WH/kids/html/home.html
Go on a virtual tour of the White House with Socks the cat and Buddy the dog. Learn about past presidents, their wives and children, and even the other pets that have lived there.

URL: http://disney.go.com/DisneyRecords
Listen to the best Disney songs and even compose your own music with Professor Notezart.

URL: http://www.hhmi.org/coolscience
Why does dust make us sneeze, and just what exactly is in a salad? This cool site for science kids answers all your questions.

URL: http://www.science-kids.com
This site has cool science facts, free games, and books for science kids to order.

CRAFTS AND COOKING

URL: http://www.myfree.com/freekid.html
Send for free cool craft kits and see what other free things you can send for from the Internet.

URL: http://www.kidscom.com
Learn about kids who live all over the world! You can also send cards, talk to other kids, find yummy recipes, and much, much more!

URL: http://www.kidsfood.com
Both fun and educational, this site has lots of information on free recipes, healthy food for kids, and even information for parents.

URL: http://www.gingerkids.com
Bake cookies with kids from all over the world on this scrumptious site!

SPORTS

URL: http://www.soccer.org
If you love soccer, you'll love this site for kids!

URL: http://www.usa-gymnastics.org
You'll flip when you log on to this site. Visit this site to see what gymnastic clubs around the country offer free classes.

URL: http://www.totalbaseball.com
Get free stats and information on your favorite teams and players.

URL: http://www.aausports.com
This is an excellent site for all amateur athletes and sports lovers.

INDEX

Activity Books, 19, 83

Activity Kit, 54, 63, 67, 77, 81, 93

Alien, 28, 39

Alligator, 73, 74

Animals, 35-6, 45, 48-49, 52, 54, 60, 62, 67, 70-74, 77, 83, 87

Awareness and Self-esteem, 80-88

Badminton, 21

Baseball, 12-14

Basketball, 10-11

Beach Ball, 58

Bike, 65, 80

Birthday, 86

Booklets, 18-20

Book Stuff, 63

Bookmarks, 60-62, 87

Bracelets, 24-26, 73

Butterflies, 40, 74

Buttons, 63, 75

Canoe, 19

Celebrities, 86

Coloring Books, 64

Comb, 87

Comic Books, 65

Dalmatians, 46

Decals, 18

Dinosaurs, 37, 44-45, 52

Dissection, 72

Earrings, 29, 32

Earth, 76, 96

Environment, 70-78, 90

Erasers, 22, 46-47, 77

Fan Packs, 10, 12-16

Fencing, 21

Flowers, 40, 47

Football, 15

Foreign Embassies, 94-95

Foreign Money, 91-92

Frames, 22, 84

Friends, 88

Glow-in-the-Dark, 34, 53

Gymnastics, 18

Hockey, 16, 41

Horses, 19, 66

Insects, 41, 48, 73-74

Internet, 97-101

Jewelry Kits, 29, 32

Jewelry, 24-32

Key Chain, 73, 96

Kayak, 19

Kite, 58

Magazines, 64-67, 71, 81

Magic, 55

Magnet, 21-22, 84

Manatee, 71

Money, 62-65, 91-92

Necklaces, 27-28

Notepads, 46, 49

Padlock, 55

Pamphlets, 19, 21, 71, 82

Paper, 48-49

Pen Pals, 72, 93

Pencils, 50-51

Pirate, 54

Play-Doh, 53

INDEX

Poetry, 61, 68
Posters, 19, 80, 83
Purse, 88, 96
Puzzles, 57
Reading, 60-68
Recycling, 77
Rings, 28-30, 77
Roller Skating, 21
Rubber Stamps, 44
Rulers, 45
Safety, 81–83

School Supplies and
  Activities, 44-58
Sea Life, 36, 46, 60
Seeds, 78
Shoelaces, 32
Soccer, 22
Sports Cards, 15, 17
Sports Tag, 22
Sports, 10-22, 38, 58
Stamps, 90
Stencil, 52

Stickers, 11-13, 21, 34-38,
  46, 57, 76, 85
Stick-on Jewelry, 31
Sun-Catchers, 54
Swimming, 18
Tattoos, 39-42, 46
Travel Games, 56-57
Trees, 75
Trolls, 27, 39
World Culture, 90-96
Writing, 53, 68, 72, 86, 93
Yo-Yo, 54

More Books Kids Will Love!

Girls to the Rescue, Book #1
Edited by Bruce Lansky

A collection of 10 folk- and fairy tales featuring courageous, clever, and determined girls from around the world. This groundbreaking book will update traditional fairy tales for girls ages 7½–13.   **order #2215**

"An enjoyable, much-needed addition to children's literature that portrays female characters in positive, active roles."
            —Colleen O'Shaughnessy McKenna, author of
            Too Many Murphys

Newfangled Fairy Tales, Book #1
Edited by Bruce Lansky

This is a collection of 10 delightful fairy tales with new twists on old stories and themes, including a contemporary King Midas who doesn't have time for his son's Little League games, a prince who refuses to marry any of the unpleasant, grumpy, and complaining young women who had slept on mattresses with peas under them, a beautiful princess who is put to sleep for 100 years because she is so cranky, and a clever princess who pays a dragon to lose a fight with a prince so she can marry the man she loves.   **order #2500**

Kids Pick the Funniest Poems

Edited by Bruce Lansky
Illustrated by Stephen Carpenter

Three hundred elementary-school kids will tell you that this book contains the funniest poems for kids—because they picked them! Not surprisingly, they chose many of the funniest poems ever written by favorites like Shel Silverstein, Jack Prelutsky, Bruce Lansky, Jeff Moss, and Judith Viorst (plus poems by lesser-known writers that are just as funny). This book is guaranteed to please children ages 6–12! **order #2410**

A Bad Case of the Giggles

Edited by Bruce Lansky
Illustrated by Stephen Carpenter

Bruce Lansky knows that nothing motivates your children to read more often than a book that makes them laugh. That's why this book will turn your kids into poetry lovers. Every poem in this book had to pass the giggle test of 600 school children. This anthology features poems by Shel Silverstein, Jack Prelutsky, Judith Viorst, and Lansky himself. (Ages 6–12).   **order #2411**

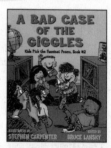

No More Homework! No More Tests!

Edited by Bruce Lansky
Illustrated by Stephen Carpenter

This is the funniest collection of poems about school by the most popular children's poets, including Shel Silverstein, Jack Prelutsky, David L. Harrison, Colin McNaughton, Kalli Dakos, Bruce Lansky, and others who know how to find humor in any subject. (Ages 6–12). **order #2414**

Kids' Outdoor Parties
by Penny Warner
Illustrated by Laurel Aiello

This book offers 35 themed outdoor parties for kids and includes invitations, costumes, decorations, games, activities, foods, cakes, favors, variations, and helpful hints. The parties are designed to be held in a backyard, at a park, or other outdoor spaces. Party ideas include Archeology Expedition with kid-sized pyramids, mummies, and mystery maps; Circus with lion taming, tightrope walking, and clown cakes; Hayride with songfests, scarecrow making, and painting with hay; and Hollywood Stunts with bicycle slalom, leapin' limbo, and other physically challenging games.   **order #6045**

Kids' Party Games and Activities
by Penny Warner
Illustrated by Kathy Rogers

This is the most complete guide to party games and activities for kids ages 2–12! It contains illustrated descriptions, instructions, rules, and trouble-shooting tips for 300 games and activities (more than triple the number in other books), including traditional and contemporary games, and simple and elaborate activities, plus ideas for outings, events, and entertainers.   **order #6095**

The Kids' Pick-a-Party Book
by Penny Warner
Illustrated by Laurel Aiello

Here are 50 creative theme parties to make birthdays and other celebrations so much fun, kids won't want to leave the party. Warner provides themed ideas for invitations, decorations, costumes, games, activities, food, and party favors to help parents make celebrations memorable and entertaining.   **order #6090**

Order Form

Quantity	Title	Author	Order No.	Unit Cost (U.S. $)	Total
	A Bad Case of the Giggles	Lansky, Bruce	2411	$16.00	
	Free Stuff for Kids, 2000 edition	Free Stuff Editors	2190	$5.00	
	Girls to the Rescue, Book #1	Lansky, Bruce	2215	$3.95	
	Girls to the Rescue, Book #2	Lansky, Bruce	2216	$3.95	
	Girls to the Rescue, Book #3	Lansky, Bruce	2219	$3.95	
	Girls to the Rescue, Book #4	Lansky, Bruce	2221	$3.95	
	Happy Birthday to Me!	Lansky, Bruce	2416	$8.95	
	Kids Are Cookin'	Brown, Karen	2440	$8.00	
	Kids' Holiday Fun	Warner, Penny	6000	$12.00	
	Kids' Party Cookbook	Warner, Penny	2435	$12.00	
	Kids' Party Games and Activities	Warner, Penny	6095	$12.00	
	Kids' Pick-A-Party Book	Warner, Penny	6090	$9.00	
	Kids Pick the Funniest Poems	Lansky, Bruce	2410	$16.00	
	Miles of Smiles	Lansky, Bruce	2412	$16.00	
	Newfangled Fairy Tales, Book #1	Lansky, Bruce	2500	$3.95	
	No More Homework! No More Tests!	Lansky, Bruce	2414	$8.00	
	Poetry Party	Lansky, Bruce	2430	$13.00	
				Subtotal	
			Shipping and Handling (see below)		
			MN residents add 6.5% sales tax		
				Total	

YES, please send me the books indicated above. Add $2.00 shipping and handling for the first book with a retail price up to $9.99, or $3.00 for the first book with a retail price over $9.99. Add $1.00 shipping and handling for each additional book. All orders must be prepaid. Most orders are shipped within two days by U.S. Mail (7–9 delivery days). Rush shipping is available for an extra charge. Overseas postage will be billed. **Quantity discounts available upon request.**

Send book(s) to:

Name _____ Phone _____

Address _____

City _____ State_____ Zip _____

Payment via:

❏ Check or money order payable to Meadowbrook Press.

❏ Visa (for orders over $10.00 only) ❏ MasterCard (for orders over $10.00 only)

Account # _____ Signature _____ Exp. Date _____

A *FREE* Meadowbrook Press catalog is available upon request.
You can also phone us for orders of $10.00 or more at 1-800-338-2232.

Mail to: Meadowbrook Press, 5451 Smetana Drive, Minnetonka, Minnesota 55343

Phone (612) 930-1100   Toll-Free 1-800-338-2232   Fax (612) 930-1940
For more information (and fun) visit our website: www.meadowbrookpress.com.